SUNSET OVER THE SCILLIES

Sunset over the Scillies

Denys Val Baker

WILLIAM KIMBER · LONDON

First published in 1975 by
WILLIAM KIMBER & CO. LIMITED
Godolphin House, 22a Queen Anne's Gate, London, SW1H 9AE

© Denys Val Baker, 1975
ISBN 0 7183 0114 5

Filmset by Specialised Offset Services Limited, Liverpool and printed and bound in Great Britain by Redwood Burn Limited, Trowbridge & Esher

Contents

*For Gill and Alan
with Love, remembering
Golden Greek days*

I

Sunset over the Scillies

Living as we do so close to Land's End, gateway to the mysterious sunset world of 'the West', it is naturally in this direction that our footsteps tend to take us when setting out for an afternoon walk. The contrast in immediate scenery alone is worth the effort: we begin at our home, an old granite mill house that seems half embedded in the fertile dark earth of Penberth Valley, a secluded and sheltered place surrounded by clambering rock gardens and cascading waterfalls and the shade of rook-filled elm trees, and we end out upon bare and bleak heather-strewn clifftops, undulating mounds of ancient stones and druidical playgrounds, forever threatened (and indeed perpetually sprayed) by the wild and foaming waves of a seething and angry Atlantic Ocean far below.

It is like passing from one universe into another: the first a snug and warm homeland, full of familiarity and peace, a kind of welcome human cosiness – the second a shatteringly alien world, brooding yet hauntingly tempting, a stark plateau that curiously combines suggestions of heaven and hell.

Geographically the change of atmosphere is made in a matter of a couple of miles or so. In fact, we do not head directly for Land's End itself, for that well popularised place is usually overwhelmed by lurid motor coaches and their somehow frantic loads of trippers, but seek a more remote part of the wandering cliffland, somewhere between the lonely finger of Cape Cornwall to the far north west and the equally lonely but squatter corner of Porthgwarra to the south, with

its solitary coastguard hut and strange red and black storm
cones, rising up like little pyramids.

To reach our chosen destination we have the pleasure of
wandering along narrow winding lanes, bordered by their
typical Cornish hedges (grass mounds of packed loam and
granite) perhaps crossing one or two typical sprawling
conclaves of farm buildings, the milking machines already
humming and great families of sad-eyed cows awaiting their
turn, and then following some increasingly pot-holed lane out
across fields of mustard or broccoli or cabbage – until the lane
peters out and we have reached that final no-man's world of
craggy cliffs and musky smelling, spring-turfed headland.

Here we curl ourselves up in some sheltered nook among
the heaps of granite and settle down to scan the horizon for
that ultimate of the romantic escaper – the Isles of Scilly. Set
about thirty miles off the toe of England, like bejewelled studs
to the mainland's shoecap, the Scillies form what is in many
ways the most mysterious of all corners of our ancient land.
Although only six are occupied the islands are said to total
more than a hundred separate entities, ranging from single
rocks or slightly larger islets like Annett, the bird sanctuary,
to large areas of land such as tropical Tresco or elongated St
Martin's, or the main island of St. Mary's.

Each one of these islands is forever impregnated with
overtones of the past: standing on some high point, such as
King Charles' Castle on Treso, and surveying the speckled
scene it is impossible not to be filled with wondrous images of
events and scenes that are long since gone. No wonder we have
been left such romantic legends: of Tristan and Iseult meeting
as lovers on the sandy islet of Sampson – of King Arthur's
knights fleeing to the Scillies for respite – of many famous
religious figures calling there, St. Patrick, Joseph of
Arimathea – even Jesus Christ himself, as a child. The islands
create that sort of highly charged atmosphere.

Not, of course, from our vantage point on the cliffs near
Land's End. Here we need an element of luck in order to see
the islands at all: for naturally on a misty day or when great
Atlantic storms have blown up clouds of sea spew and foam,

then the horizon is drastically curtailed and the visibility, far from reaching thirty miles, may not extend much past the two-mile distant Longship's lighthouse, and a few shadowy shapes of ocean liners passing by in a maelstrom of white-capped waves.

Sometimes we may have deliberately taken our walk in such conditions, happy enough to gaze out upon the majestic seas and breathtaking views, with huge waves curling up nearly to the top of the cliffs – remembering on such occasions, with vivid horror, days such as a bleak Sunday when a small Danish cargo vessel trapped on the Armed Knight rocks, was relentlessly pounded to death by the huge waves. Wrecks around the Land's End area are still too common, and we have never forgotten another occasion (which the reader may remember from pictures in the national newspapers) when a French crabber had lain for two whole days crucified on the rocks, awash by the sea, all hope given up – and suddenly a hand emerged from the top of the wheelhouse window and waved pathetically. As a result, a Culdrose helicopter came racing over and a daring rescue was carried out of three French seamen who had been trapped all that time in their wheelhouse.

However, normally, with luck and decent weather conditions, we would have some reasonable chance of seeing, from our cliffland vantage point, the ultimate objective of our afternoon stroll ... the more so if that stroll was made fairly late in the day, when the sun had begun to sink over the western horizon illuminating the distant cloudy outlines. Then we would begin our scanning of the far horizon by staring over to the south western edges, tracing a line until one of us would cry out, 'The Wolf!' – and there, standing eerily and in astonishing loneliness, like a single pencil end, would be the high shape of the Wolf Lighthouse, built on a rock about eight miles off Land's End, an extra guardian for incoming and outgoing Channel steamers.

Once we had established the position of the Wolf then we only had to follow the arc round about another thirty degrees and at last we would have the stupendous visual pleasure of seeing the Isles of Scilly rearing up against the bright shafts of golden light, mysterious humps of magical other-worldiness.

Weirdest experience of all, most magical moment of all, would be on some wintry afternoon when daylight faded early, and the sun happened to have acquired that deep bright redness sometimes feared by seamen. We have never forgotten some of those early evening sunsets over the Scillies when the entire skyline seemed aflame with strange shapes and images, great canopies of clouds rising and falling like smoke from some witches cauldrons, lurid colour schemes splitting the sky in all directions – and there on the very edge of the horizon itself, illuminated in a most ghostly fashion by the huge red-orange ball of the sun, would be those strange silhouettes, the long plateau of St. Mary's, the distant humps of St. Agnes and Bryher, and perhaps, already winking ahead of the final dusk, the bright light of Round Island Lighthouse. Magical memories, indeed, are those of the sunsets over the Scillies.

When we originally came to visit the 'Fortunate Isles' (as every romantic should whether living in Cornwall or not) we found them just as fascinating as their sunset images suggested, perhaps more so. The mere approach is magic itself, even if made by the mundane helicopter from Penzance – in which case they lay splayed out like a jewelled necklace in the foaming sea below – but more so still if coming by sea, on the *Scillonian* steaming confidently between Spanish Ledge and the Bartholomew Buoy, with St. Agnes on one hand, and Pendennis Point on the other, suddenly swinging into St. Mary's Sound and edging up to the steamer pier at St. Mary's. Islands, of course, are notorious inspirers of that romantic feeling, and there is certainly an inescapable romance about coming up to St. Mary's from the open sea, finding haven, stepping ashore into that strange new tight-knit world.

Perhaps we were especially fortunate in that many of our visits to the Scillies were made in our own boat, *Sanu*. Once we had acquired this old former fishing vessel it was only natural that we should embark on the comparatively short crossing to

St. Mary's. Rather comically in view of our subsequent voyages – 1500 miles to Sweden in one direction, 2000 miles to the Med in another – I can remember how nervous we were that first time as we left the shelter of Newlyn and Mount's Bay and hopefully set our compass course 275° for Pendennis Point. For, on that first trip at any rate, since visibility at sea-level is nothing like that at cliff top level, for a long time we could not see the Scillies and were travelling blind. Then what relief when someone called out 'land ahead' – and there were those soon-to-be-familiar humps. With what pride we came into the Sound and up to the pier head, tying up along-side one of the skin-diver's boats just below where the *Scillonian* berthed.

Skin-diving was actually the reason for our first trip to the Scillies. It was the time of the great hullabaloo about the finding of the wreckage of Admiral Cloudesley Shovel's *Association* flagship, which had been wrecked in fog with the loss of two thousand lives. For centuries the great hulk had lain somewhere off the Gilstone Reef in about twenty fathoms, but latterly numerous parties of divers had been vying with each other to reclaim the treasure. The man who ultimately captured the prize was a Penzance restaurant owner, Rowland Morris, a remarkable man who gave his own vivid account of the experience in *Island Adventure*. But these were pre-Rowland Morris days, and when a friend, Doug Rowe, one of the professional skin divers who was later to work with Morris, suggested going out to the Scillies so that he could take a look around for wrecks, we jumped at the excuse.

We stayed over several summer weekends, with *Sanu* anchored most of the time in the very narrow strait between Tresco and Bryher – an area so shallow in parts that when there are exceptionally high and low tides so much land is uncovered that a farmer on Bryher can drive a tractor across to Tresco! We still look back with great pleasure on those early days. Usually we would berth for a night or two at St. Mary's, sampling the more mundane delights of that 'main' island, one of the cosiest being having a drink in the famous

Mermaid Tavern, just off the main quay.

Most of the life of St. Mary's is centred on that quay on which every morning there is a great hustle and bustle awaiting the arrival of the *Scillonian*, due in soon after twelve following its daily crossing from Penzance. First there would be unloading of passengers, perhaps five hundred of them, sometimes looking pale and wan if it had been a rough crossing; next came urgent supplies from the mainland, ranging from a hundred gas cylinders to a motor lorry or a horse-box. Once emptied the big white steamer – with its exceptionally low draught of ten foot to enable it to berth at St. Mary's – was soon filled up, perhaps with flowers or vegetables. At such times the harbour was an attractive place, full of colour and life, especially as many of the trippers would be in process of climbing in the long motor launches for quick tours of the off-islands.

It was the off-islands that we finally came to like most, especially around *Sanu's* anchorage off Tresco. Here we would land by dinghy at New Grimsby Quay, then take the wandering pathway that criss-crossed the lovely tropical vegetation of what was often known as 'the Major's Island' – for Tresco was leased by the Duchy of Cornwall to the Dorrien-Smith family, of whom the head then was Major Dorrien-Smith, one of whose ancestors had been responsible for reviving the flower trade of the Scillies. (There is a famous story of the then Governor, seeing endless poverty for the islands and determined to find a solution, sending a single hatbox of daffodils to Covent Garden in 1865 – and receiving £1 for them).

Tresco Abbey and its fabulous tropical gardens are the centre piece of Tresco, and we loved wandering about, smelling the fragrant perfumes of oleanders and hibiscus, staring in amazement at such oddities as the huge banana and fig trees and many other testaments to the truth of the claim that the shores of the Isles of Scilly unlike any other part of Britain, are washed by the warm waters of the Gulf Stream.

When we were tired of wandering around we might sit down for an ice cream or a drink in the gardens of 'Valhalla', that continued prosperity of fishing, the nineteenth century Scillonians built up an immense skilful trade in pilotage. Sometimes as many as three hundred ships might seek shelter in the Roads from gales, and this meant lucrative business for the Scillonians' ten pilot boats, each with a crew of eight men. Today, of course there is not the same demand, and I think there are only two pilots – but the Scillies' long tradition of service at sea has been nobly preserved in the lifeboat service operated by the Royal National Lifeboat Institute. I doubt if any lifeboat around the British Isles is called out as frequently as the Isles of Scilly boat – nor if any other boat has carried out so many dramatic rescues.

Sometimes these rescues take place far out in the wild waters of the Atlantic, perhaps succouring the crew of a Spanish fishing boat in distress by the Seven Stones reef (where the *Torrey Canyon* struck and sank), or towing in a crippled Belgian or French trawler, or maybe a dismasted English yacht cruising home from France – and sometimes the rescues are on the very doorstep, involving intricate manoeuvering in dangerous shoal waters, as when the lifeboat came to our own help in the narrow sea between Bryher and Tresco, with sharp fanged rocks looming in every direction. This is the time when lives literally depend on the fantastic knowledge of local waters that comes naturally to men such as Matt Lethbridge, coxswain of the Isles of Scilly lifeboat.

Life in the Scillies is so dominated by the sea in all its needs that all our own memories of the islands are equally dominated. Fortunately for us the sea's wrathfulness was usually muted, and most of the time we lay peacefully at anchor, sunbathing on *Sanu's* broad decks or diving over the side into crystal clear waters. When Doug Rowe was with us many of the family had a go at the exciting new art of skin-diving. Doug himself was an expert diver, and later on when searching for the *Association* he regularly went down to a hundred feet and more. At first Doug had hopes of training our son Stephen to follow in his wake so to speak! There was a momentous occasion when a somewhat nervous Stephen disappeared beneath the water one side of *Sanu* — and re-appeared quite a while later the other side. This, alas, was his one and only official skin-dive, for he proved to be one of the unlucky ones whose sinuses responded loudly to such treatment, and had to give up thoughts of finding treasures deep under the water.

Doug, on the other hand, went from strength to strength, personally finding ducats and other valuable coins, and helped to recover much of the *Association's* cannons and other armaments. After it was all over he had changed from a part-time skin-diver to an ultra professional who had earned so much money that he built himself a marvellous all steel yacht in which, with his wife Sue, he later sailed out to the Mediterranean.

Our own expeditions were usually more modest affairs, and invariably made in an old Zodiac inflatable we carried on *Sanu*. In this sturdy craft, with its incredibly shallow draft of a mere few inches, we were able to explore many of the more fascinating of the uninhabited parts of the Scillies. Our favourite spot for a picnic was the island of Sampson, a sandy hillock in the sea just off Bryher with grassy slopes and the ruins of an old house. We used to beach the boat, climb up the sands, eat our picnic lunches, and then dream away the days. Jess and I would often feel drawn to Sampson, and once got very excited to hear that there might be a possibility of renting the island. I have always felt that would indeed have been a very appropriate home for the vast and wandering Val Baker family, an island in the Scillies! We even went so far as to write to the Duchy of Cornwall making an offer to rent Sampson. Alas, our hopes were dashed, politely but firmly – lack of water was one of the reasons given, I remember – and we had to be satisfied with picnics and dreams.

One of our close friends, Biddy Picard, has in recent years acquired the Scilly habit, and spends many weeks of each year staying on the small offshore island of St. Agnes. Here in a cosy little community of about 50 people, she reckons to have found a peace and quiet missing even on mainland Cornwall, and certainly from all she tells us there is something very attractive about life on a beautiful small island, where the village centre is a former lighthouse, turned into a guest house, a few other cottages, and now a small pub. St. Agnes is one of those places where neighbour just *has* to help neighbour: for instance there is no proper harbour, boats have to be run up on the beach and unloaded quickly, all mucking in, before the tide turns.

Although only a couple of miles from St. Mary's the sea between the two islands can often get up so rough that communications can be completely cut off. It is not, of course, a sea of the incredible size of some around the Bishop Rock Lighthouse, at the north end of the Scillies, but bad enough. I have often envied Biddy snug evenings tucked in her cottage on St. Agnes, listening to the boom and hiss of the sea, safe among friends and protective rocks and cliffs ... and wished I too had a home on the Scillies.

Mind you, reality might not be quite as romantic as dreaming. As with so many islands, one gathers that the general attitude of the Scillonians today, as in the past, is a little reactionary, especially towards the hordes of visitors that flock over every summer. Many young people (generally with long hair) have found themselves met at the harbour when they get off the *Scillonian* and more or less encouraged to leave again! This happened to our own son Martin, who was most indignant as he had been officially sent over to caretake aboard *Sanu* while we were all back at our home in St. Ives!

In the same way one could imagine that life in the Scillies, if you fell foul of local opinion, could be a little difficult. But then when all is said and done, there remains the most marvellous seascape cum landscape – whenever human frailty disappointed, one could always take one of those beautiful walks, like the one round Pendennis Head and out along the wild cliffs, coming back down the gentle slopes to Portressa beach – or better still across the wild Tresco moors leading to Cromwell Castle, looking out upon the ominously named Hangman's Isle.

Best of all, of course, if you are on the Scillies, is to take to the water itself, and wander delightfully among the craggy islets, calling at such remote spots as Gugh – a little island

adjoining St. Agnes, joined to it by a causeway that is covered
by the sea each high tide. Here, by the way, just as I was
writing this book, the two solitary houses were sold on tender
for a sum of £46,000 – which is not bad, surely, for the access
to an island of your own! St. Martin's is another delightful
place to call in by boat, as we have often done, landing on the
long incredibly white bathing beach.

A painter friend, Tony O'Malley, stays frequently at St.
Martin's, and from there has painted many striking abstract
interpretations of Scillonian grandeur. It would be interesting,
no doubt, to collect an anthology of work by artists of all kinds
who have been impressed by the Scillies – Tennyson, Dickens,
among writers, Turner, Rowlandson among painters come to
mind.

George Eliot was another author who spent weeks at St.
Mary's coining some vivid phrases in her notebooks:
'Rectangular crevices, the edges of which have been rounded
by the weather, give many of the granite masses a resemblance
of wool or copper heaped on each other' is one: another, 'the
mushroomed-shaped mass often lying poised on the summits
of more cubical boulders'. It would be a long time, she
concluded, before she would forget visions of 'a heap of white
boulders, sometimes remarkable perfect ovals like the eggs of
some monstrous bird'.

George Eliot's reason for visiting the Scillies was not a
literary one, however. With her lifelong partner, George
Henry Lewes, she had come over from the mainland and
settled into lodgings near the Post Office (the rooms for 14/- a
week with 18p a day extra for a fire!) in order to do some
serious research. The morning after their arrival, armed with
a chisel and can the two visitors were off along the storm-
swept coast searching for zoophytes and molluscs – in fact
Lewes was at that time working on a book, *Sea-Side Studies*,
which catalogues marine life. Tropical plants, marine life,
mineralogy – the beaches are rich with jade, chalcedony,
amethyst and topaz – are all magnets that draw innumerable
distinguished visitors to the Scillies. The islands offer many
natural treasures besides the braided cannon and valuable lead

little open air museum of ship's figureheads. Staring at some of these handsome models we would vow that one day we would have such a proud emblem on the bow of *Sanu* ... so far we have not achieved this ambition, but we live in hopes! Many of the Scilly figureheads belonged to famous schooners of the day, and served to jog one's historical memory – as did the famous collection of photographs of past shipwrecks which adorn the walls of the New Inn on Tresco.

Quite possibly a photograph of *Sanu* is now among these, for once we, too, were wrecked (as I have described in *Spring at Land's End*) but in the earlier times I am remembering *Sanu* always laid placidly at her anchorage, close by Major Dorrien-Smith's own elegant motor yacht, and we had no problems. The only time we had to have a small repair job done, on the stern land, we took the boat over to St. Mary's and beached her at the top end of the harbour and the work was efficiently handled by the island carpenter from whom we learned much of the intricacies of the community life of the island, with everyone ready to help one another. This sense of community must linger from very ancient times, for no such isolated area could have survived without a common will – and what's more survived through so many vicissitudes. Those early days were described once for me in a special article the historian Miss M. Mortimer wrote for the *Cornish Review*.

After the fall of Rome the Dark Ages were very dark in Scilly. As late as the time of Henry VIII his surveyor Leyland observed: 'There be few men willing to inhabit these islands for all the plentie, for robbers by sea take their catail of force'. Scilly remained a happy hunting ground for pirates and robbers throughout the Elizabethan era, when the Lord High Admiral of England himself was executed for piracy centred around the islands. But after the Armada and the Civil War (Scilly was the last Royalist outpost) life gradually improved. Eighteenth century writers give a pleasant picture of life in Scilly and of its prosperity, perhaps increased by the garrison of some 600 men in Star Castle.

Borlase described the plentiful crops and fruits. Troutbeck observed that even the poorest need never go in need for fish, barley, bread and potatoes, and lists a formidable number of trades flourishing on St. Mary's, not only butcher, baker, brewer, cooper, weaver and tailor, but shipwright, joiner, mason, smith, glazier and barber. The long disaster of the Napoleonic Wars broke upon this pleasant scene and reduced Scilly to near famine ... the misery of the islanders being partly due to suppression of smuggling by which they had previously profited. However charity revived the fishing industry by the gifts of fish cellars, boats and tackle, and by the eighteen-sixties Scilly had become the headquarters of western mackerel fishing. Meanwhile on land the rise and fall of one major occupation after another makes fascinating study for the economic historian. Gone are the straw plaiters, the rope makers, thatchers, woolcombers, spinners, hat and corset makers. Kelp-making became a widespread occupation, each family staking out its claim in special rocks for fetching the precious weed. The 18th century books are full of litigation between indignant islanders on the subject of oreweed poaching. By the 1840's the trade had been lost to the Northern Islands and to Spain, but as if to make amends for this, the story runs that in 1838 the master of a Spanish vessel gave a Scillonian lad some seed potatoes. They were found to grow quickly and well, so faced with the destruction of the kelp trade the adaptable Scillonians turned to a new and highly profitable trade. Alas, by the end of the fifties England had become a Free Trade country, and the potatoes went the way of kelp, to Spain ...

It was after this that the Scillonians turned to boat building. The boats were small because of the heavy dues that had to be paid on boats over 60 tons, but the Scillonian 'fifty-niners' became world famous, many of them crossing the Atlantic. Along with the development of shipbuilding, and the

II
Water, Water Everywhere

Many things may be said to have varied in our life at the Mill House, now in its third year, but one item has remained absolutely constant and that is water. It is a case of water, water everywhere. It begins one end of the property where the river comes snaking down from Crean Bottoms, sluicing under a stout stone parapet and then irrigating the lawns and shrubberies and woods – and it ends in a far corner where the stream tumbles away under a stone bridge to widen its way through the next garden and then across pretty daffodil fields until it reaches Penberth and the sea.

In between this beginning and end some of the water takes a diversionary course via a man-made leat in order to rise up behind the house and provide the power that once used to operate the great wooden wheel which still protrudes from the south facing wall. In the olden days the water in the leat used to turn the wooden wheel whose motion in turn operated intricate machinery in the wheel-room, which charged batteries and provided free electricity. Although Stephen, and indeed many other enthusiasts, have announced that they would soon get the old wheel working again somehow progress has been slow. A few new spokes, two or three massive wooden arms, a hopeful lubrication – and there the matter rests. Meantime the water continues to race by. It is this same water which also provides the supply of drinking water for the family – and thereby hangs a hypochrondriacal story!

When we first moved into the Mill House we noted that the previous inhabitants had drunk the stream water for some twenty-eight years and were still alive to tell the tale. Nevertheless, just to be on the safe side I asked officials of the local council health department out to come and test the water, and in due course had it pronounced bacteriologically OK, so long as we passed it through a ceramic filter. At the same time, while they were out, I got the water officials to test water from an old well up in our field ... the report on this was that though the water was satisfactory it had a very high acid content and should not be used in lead pipes. Upon the assumption that if lead pipes could disintegrate from the acid in the well water this liquid was hardly likely to be especially kind to the lining of our stomachs, we went on drinking the waters of our own river.

At first all was well, then gradually as the months went by my always dormant hypochondria began bubbling away – literally in the form of a continually disturbed stomach. Casting around in my mind for some explanation – conveniently ignoring such delicacies as Cornish cream, rich cheeses and my beloved wines – I came to the conclusion that the most obvious culprit, the cause of my abdominal distress, could only be our water supply.

'But you've had it tested,' said Jess impatiently. 'Remember? The man came out and said it was perfectly OK through a filter.'

'That's all very well. You must admit my bad stomach has only really developed since we came here and started drinking this water.'

It seemed to me there was no gainsaying this simple and logical argument, and I began brooding on the implications. No longer could I lightly fill up a kettle to make a morning cup of coffee – every time I turned on the tap and watched the suspect water dribbling out of the filter I began to feel increasingly worried. What's more, if I went up the valley and looked at the water in the leat entrance my doubts grew considerably. Often, after rain, the water turned a dark and muddy colour – sometimes, too, it appeared to be covered with a kind of white foam that looked suspiciously like detergent. We knew that from its source to our house the stream passed mainly through open moorland, so there must be some rational sort of explanation – all the same it wasn't an encouraging sight. Supposing ... ? Well, it didn't need much imagination to conjure up all sorts of horrible ideas.

'Isn't there some *dreadful* thing you can get from water that's been contaminated by sheep? Liver fluke, that's it!'

'That's an animal disease.'

'Maybe, but all the same – '

'And anyway, you know there aren't any sheep in West Cornwall.'

'Nonsense.'

'All right – *where* have you seen sheep around here?'

Unable to ignore such a direct challenge I spent the next few days casting a searching eye around the surrounding fields. I saw cows and pigs and horses and hens and dogs and donkeys and goats – oh, and geese and ducks and drakes and even one or two peacocks – but never anywhere did I see a single sheep.

'There,' said Jess smugly.

'Well, anyway, liver fluke is only one thing. What about – *chemicals?*'

'Do you seriously suggest people deliberately put chemicals in the stream?'

It did seem a bit far-fetched. All the same it was a fact, I knew, that farmers were using more and more chemical fertilisers. Come heavy rain and surely some of these would be washed down into the stream? Yes, it all made sense. Disturbing sense.

I began to like the look of our water supply less and less. Possibly in keeping with my thoughts my stomach distress became more and more bothersome. One day I made my momentous announcement.

'I am *not* going to drink our stream water any more.'

Jess shrugged.

'Oh, well, I hope you enjoy lugging heavy buckets all the way from the well.'

I looked superior.

'The well water is highly acid. That would be even more damaging. I am *not* going to drink the well water, *either*.'

Looking back I suppose it all sounds a little arbitrary, but bear in mind that I had been worrying around this problem for weeks, even months. Now I felt the need for some action – dramatic action.

First I demanded a visit from a Water Board Engineer to explain to me why we could not be put on mains water. One wet and windy day a sad little man with a curiously defeated air about him trudged down the lane. He looked around him and heaved a resigned and meaningful sigh.

'I'll tell you why you can't have mains here, guvnor. In the first place, it could cost you anything up a thousand pounds to bring it from the main road – have you got a thousand pounds handy?'

Before I could speak he went on.

'And in the second place, the only other way would be for you to have a sub-section run down to you from Lady Bolitho's farm up on top of the hill, that's the only place remotely near otherwise – and shall I tell you something? The water supply there is already insufficient, in the summer they often run dry. If you were connected you'd have to take second turn, so to speak – in the summer *you'd* certainly be without water, half the time!'

The Water Board man went off shaking his head sagely, and I was left literally to my own water resources. Seeing my look of discomfort Jess tried to jolly me out of what she patently regarded as my obsession.

'Look, be logical. *I* drink the water, don't I? Stephen used to drink the water when he was here – Genevieve drinks the water when she's here. Why don't *we* all have bad tummies?' She shook her head. 'It must be something else.'

Doggedly I shook my head.

'It's the water. I know it is. It must be.'

I retired to my office and had a long think. Shortly after I came out my face beaming.

'I've thought what to do. I'll buy two of those large plastic containers – you know the sort they have at Pratt's, five gallons they hold – I'll fill them up with good water and stick to that.'

It seemed a simple enough idea at first. I bought the containers brought them home in the car and stood them proudly on the kitchen table.

'There, they'll hold ten gallons of water. How much do you think a human being drinks a week? Would they last a week –?' I did some quick calculations. 'Oh yes, surely. Maybe two weeks if I'm careful.' Suddenly struck by a thought I looked at Jess uneasily. 'Or – would *you* be wanting to –?'

'Oh, no, no, don't worry about me. I am quite happy poisoning myself with the old stream. Don't worry, I'll let you know if I feel like a change.'

Jess paused and then looked at the empty containers.

'Er, *where* are you going to fill them?'

It is surprising how often the simplest of apparent problems proves to be the most difficult to solve. Hitherto I simply hadn't thought about the business of getting water *into* the containers. Now as I did, all sorts of snags loomed up.

The most obvious course would be to call in our nearest neighbours and ask if they would mind if I filled the cans from their taps. Unfortunately, as is too often the case in remote country districts, relations with our nearest and indeed only neighbours were not of the best, ever since a period when Stephen and his friends used to play jazz into the early hours of the morning. Reluctantly, I abandoned this line of approach.

When I began to think a little further afield a quick solution continued to evade me. Alas, our next nearest neighbours consisted of a market-gardener-cum-bird-breeder with a posse of dogs who barked around our feet every time we passed his house ... and who had not exactly struck up a friendship with our own dog.

Depressed by such memories I quickly slurred over other possibilities, an anonymous painter at one house, an elderly and apparently equally seclusive baronet in another. For their own reasons, as far as we were concerned, they obviously preferred to keep themselves to themselves – and who could blame them? All the same, not good bets for a cosy water-filling session!

My mind travelled onwards, considerably onwards, as much as three miles to St. Buryan where spasmodically we dealt with one or two tradesmen, but otherwise did not really know anyone on terms that permitted calling in casually with my two five gallon water drums.

'Buryas Bridge Garage!' I said suddenly. 'They're always very friendly. I'll fill up there next time I get some petrol.'

Anxious to be filling up my cans I did not wait until I actually needed petrol but drove over the same afternoon and had my tank filled up completely, quite an expensive business.

'Oh, by the way,' I said casually, handing over several pound notes. 'I wonder if you'd mind if I just filled up a couple of water cans?'

'Course not. Go ahead, guvnor. The tap's over there.'

Triumphant, I got out of the car, opened the boot, brought out my containers and started lugging them over to the tap.

'By the way,' called out the garage man, in slight concern. 'You won't be *drinking* the water will you? You see we've only got stream water here – all right for filling radiators and washing up – but, well you know, it might not be safe for drinking.'

I drove home in silence, and remained hunched into an unfriendly mood for the rest of the day. Jess probably put it down to my tummy playing up. The trouble was that by now determination to fill my water tanks was beginning to take precedence over all other problems, like work –.or even my tummy.

I decided to sleep on the problem and hope I would wake up with a new solution. Rather surprisingly I did.

'I've got it! I remember now. There's a public lavatory on the front at Penzance, that's got a big tap in one corner. I can fill the cans there.'

As I drove into Penzance the next day I nodded to myself with quiet satisfaction. Of course – I remembered now, this was often a method I obtained water for *Sanu* when we were travelling about remoter places. Even if there was not a piped supply near the quay there was usually a public toilet with a tap in a corner.

I drove along the front, parked the car, took out my cans and – feeling just a little self conscious as obviously it was not normal for a man to carry two large water cans into a public toilet in Penzance – walked into the toilets. Yes, there in the corner was the tap.

I went over. The pipe came up to a point, and there was *one* part of the tap – but someone had removed the lever with which you turned the tap on or off. I stared in utter disbelief – but that's how it was, right enough. Somewhere there would be a part which, if applied, would allow water to come out. But where was it? I looked around hopelessly. There was no attendant, no sign of the missing part.

I went across to a small door marked 'Washing Room', paid my coin, went in. Ah ... here were two wash-basins with taps. I picked up one of the cans, and then slowly put it down again. There was no possible way in which I could get such a large can into the basin and under the tap. I tried – my God, I tried. But it was a physical impossibility.

By now, one or two men had come into the toilets, performed their duties and gone out again – all had given me rather queer looks. Unhappily I picked up my cans and went out myself.

I had another try at a public lavatory at the other end of Penzance, but without any better results. By now the afternoon was passing away quite quickly and I had several urgent shopping problems, so I turned my attention to these for the moment. Then, when these tasks were out of the way, I had a new brainwave. I would drive down to the Mask Pottery, the pottery business which Jess used to run some years ago, and which her partner had carried on. Yes, that was it. Be nice to have a chat with the girls ...

I drove up outside the pottery, started to get out of the car – and then froze. The pottery was unlit, the doors locked. They had all gone home for the day.

Defeated and dejected I got into the car and drove all the

way home. When Jess tried to question me I snapped at her
rudely. We had supper in a gloomy silence. It was altogether a
very unfriendly evening.

The next day, when I was still in a mood of dejection, Jess
said her friend Jackie Durrant, who had started her own
pottery out at Pendeen, had asked her to come over and give
some advice over a kiln which had broken down.

'I thought we might drive over. It would make a break –
cheer her up.'

I shrugged morosely.

'All right.'

We drove over, taking the road past the windy Land's End
airport and down through the grey huddled town of St. Just,
then out along the moorland road to Pendeen. Jackie's pottery
had been set up in a former cow house, right on the edge of the
busy holiday route from Land's End to St. Ives. It should be a
good selling position. Inside we were most impressed by the
work she had done, laying out a first class pottery, complete
with wheel, shelves, pug-mills, dozens of bins, a huge gas kiln,
and a smaller electric kiln, whose elements were now all black
and broken.

'I'll soon fix that,' said Jess cheerfully. 'They're usually
wired in sections.'

While Jess went to work I wandered round the pottery
examining some of Jackie's work, admiring one or two big
coiled pots. Suddenly I came round a corner and found a
small electric cooker, an enamel sink and above it – a tap. A
tap!

I spun round and called out excitedly.

'Jackie! Do you have mains water?'

'Er – why yes, Denys.'

'All right for drinking?'

'Yes, of course.'

'Mind if I fill up a couple of containers?'

Jackie looked at me oddly.

'Why, no.' She laughed a little uncertainly. 'Help yourself.'

I rushed out to the car, got my two containers and put them
under the tap, filling them right to the brim. Then, with a

feeling of triumph, I carried them out and put them in the boot of the car.

'Thank God for that,' said Jess with feeling when I came back into the pottery. 'He's been driving me around the bend over this blessed water.'

When two hours later I arrived back at the Mill House I was at first somewhat discomfited to find that one of the containers had a leak and was half empty – but the other was full. At least I had made a beginning. I had my own alternative water supply.

The saga was by no means over. It was not always convenient to drive fourteen miles out of our way to Jackie's pottery and back – and though once or twice I did manage to catch the Mask Pottery open I became a little put off when the girls there started grumbling about the 'funny taste' in *their* water. After one or two other tentative approaches had somehow proved unsatisfactory, too, I began calling in at a wine shop and purchasing bottled mineral water – at 15p a bottle! This proved to be pure and sparkling and very pleasant to drink, but at the rate of two bottles a day, a financial impossibility. Nevertheless for some considerable time I persisted with a combination of expensive bottled mineral water and fortuitous fillings up of my water containers at friends' houses. I used to feel a little awkward about making special visits, but devised a system of being sure to have my cans with me any time we were invited out for a meal. Then as we entered, and before our eager hosts had a chance to remove our coats and settled us down for a drink, I would smoothly run through my 'Mind-if-I-just-fill-up-one-of-my-water-cans?' routine. After a while I think they all got quite used to this mild eccentricity.

Looking back I realise how much water has dominated our lives, or certainly my life. It is funny how one misses a point until it becomes central to one's consideration – then the evidence is embarrassingly everywhere. Almost the first home I ever lived in at Cornwall was set on a headland on the North Coast and so surrounded by water that huge waves would often send spray over the rooftop. Before long I was living in a cottage above Sennen Cove where two thirds of the view consisted of the wild Atlantic ocean. Later on at St. Ives we lived at a long low house on Porthmeor Beach where the water often did not wait for us to go to it, but came bursting through our kitchen doors, flooding half the house.

And then what about our previous home, the Old Sawmills at Fowey? If ever there was a water dominated spot, that was surely it. In fact there was so much water around the Sawmills that you could literally only get to the house by means of a boat along the River Fowey. There was no road, only a narrow railway track running along the side of the river – along which at a pinch we could walk, though often in the dark you were quite likely to tumble over into the water.

At the Sawmills the house was set at the head of a small creek which was completely tidal. At one stage of the day the house stood alone and forlorn surrounded by a sea of mud – six hours later you would have the most breathtaking and beautiful view of an ancient house apparently floating on the surface of a serene lake. Ah, how beautiful that all was, indeed. No wonder we would spend hours sitting down by the quayside watching the calm water slowly washing the leafy shores. How we savoured moments when someone in a rowing boat turned under the railway bridge and come sculling across the water, leaving a white frothy wake behind them. Yes, that water element of the Sawmills was exceptionally beautiful and peaceful – even when hordes of our teenage children's friends would descend for a weekend, light a bonfire and play their musical instruments long into the night.

But at the Sawmills, as at Mill House, there was another more practical side to the water problem – and one just as baffling. There the water supply had also been a stream running down through Colvethick Woods, although the actual system was slightly different to the Mill House. At the Sawmills, too, there had once been a water wheel and a leat and so on: over the years, however, this had fallen into disrepair, and some intermediary owner had dug trenches and laid a long water pipe from the stream right down to water tanks just above the house. These tanks filled up and supplied the water system.

Once again an unorthodox water system – with its own, as you might say, built-in problems. The worst one from our point of view was that no matter how clear we kept the stream end of the water pipe – using gauze and wire covering and heaven knows what else – inevitably the long piping used to get blocked. Fortunately there were one or two joins on the way, in the parts that were not buried, and if there was a blockage it usually used to be a case of tramping through the undergrowth, opening one or two of these joins, poking about with long wires and gradually freeing the passage.

Sometimes, however, things were not as simple as that. Obstructions could get so far down the pipe that they became beyond reach of our lengths of wire – they might even travel right up to the entrance to the water tank by the house. Here, fortunately, there was a considerable reduction in the width of the connections – otherwise who knows what we might have found swimming around in our water tank! On several occasions when we uncoupled the joins on to the water tank we found, stuck in the pipe, a live wriggling eel! Once there was one at least a foot long. How it had made such a journey – where it thought it was going – how were we to get it out – all these were problems apparently without answers. In the end by a most complicated series of manoeuvres we did manage to get the eel out – but by then, understandably, it had died of shock.

Amusingly, I hear that the water saga of the Sawmills has carried on momentum (just as no doubt it will here). Apparently Tony Cox, the new owner – another romantic like myself who bought the house from us in order to set up a recording studio in the peace and quiet of Colvethick Valley – decided to solve the water problem once and for all by installing mains water. Since the nearest mains water connection was at a farm high up the wooded valley, possibly some two miles away, the mind boggles at the cost of this operation. Permission was finally obtained to run black PVC piping through the woods, though it all had to be buried, and

ultimately at long last mains water was brought to the
Sawmills – though not, as can be imagined, without many
formidable structural problems en route.

I don't suppose, however, that having water by such a
conventional method as via the mains had in general had any
effect in reducing the eccentric nature of life at the Sawmills. I
was always glad that someone after our own heart took over
our old home ... and like to think of our former familiar glades
resounding to the lively voices and music of some of today's
leading pop groups. What my unlamented neighbours of
nearby Golant make of it all, heaven knows!

Where there's water, in huge quantities, then usually sooner
or later there will be rats. In our days at the Old Sawmills we
were regularly plagued by enormous water rats that came up
out from alongside the river and made onslaughts on our
chalets, even sometimes the main house. Now at the Mill
House, just as I was about settling my own water problems,
the big autumnal rains brought not merely the usual flooding,
but also the arrival of rats. The trouble now was that, whereas
the Sawmills had been built high up and generally beyond the
ken of rats, the Mill House is built low down and our kitchen
floor is literally just above long sloping muddy ground leading
originally from the stream, and down which, inevitably, rats
find their way. Unfortunately for us they proved to be a very
domestically orientated breed, who preferred exploring the
back of the kitchen and among the mysterious regions of our
cupboards ... so that one day we were sitting having a meal at
the table, heard a faint noise, looked across and saw two lively
little beasts scuttling along the edge of the sink unit!

Enough was enough, Jess decided, even though from her
days as a medical student she remembered affectionately the
white rats on which she used to perform intelligence tests.
That is the trouble with rats, they are the most intelligent of
creatures, and cannot be easily outwitted. So the only thing is
to call in the Rat Man, that strange figure out of childhood
memories.

Our experience has been that Rat Men, perhaps by the very
nature of their occupation, tend to be rather eccentric

individuals. Mostly they seem to be lost in the limbo of a private and personal relationship with the rats, coming to look upon them knowingly almost as old friends, understanding and appreciating their ways. This was the case now with our new Rat Man, who was up to all the rats' tricks, and went round patiently laying out their doom.

Not that rat catching was a one sided affair, as he assured us over the inevitable cup of tea. No, there were many hazards to his profession. And he told us a gruesome story of a colleague who used to boast about his immunity to catching infection – even putting rat poison in his mouth and eating it scornfully. One day he was taken to hospital, and in two weeks was dead, from the dreaded Weil's disease. We could not help thinking of that story a few weeks later, when the most pungent and awful smell began to pervade our kitchen. There could only be one explanation, a dead rat somewhere under the floorboards. I had to spend a whole day laboriously uprooting half the floor before I finally found the maggot ridden body and shovelled it away into a sack. Ah, the country life, so romantic!

We breathed sighs of relief when finally the Rat Man came again and pronounced the Mill House 'clean', and we were able to get on with other things.

However, we decided not to let our watery experiences go by unnoticed, and to do something we had been talking about for a long time – go along to the next local meeting of the Friends of the Earth, one of several bodies concerned with conservation which have recently sprung up all over the British Isles.

For anyone who has any thought about the future of this planet the activities of such bodies present a slender lifeline of sanity. At least let us *start* thinking about our environment, what we have done and are doing to ruin it – and, at least in small personal ways, try and make some sort of contribution. Perhaps we in the country have a special opportunity – but in other ways, people in towns can make even greater contributions. Either way it behoves us all to think around such problems otherwise even the 'water, water everywhere' with which I began this chapter may become so contaminated that not even filters will work, and our whole world will become disastrously and finally polluted.

III

A Wife for All Seasons

When not arguing about our water supply Jess and I were quite likely to be arguing about something else – almost anything in fact. For twenty-five years we have spent a good deal of quite pleasurable time setting up each other's Aunt Sallies and expertly knocking them down again. Invariably Jess has the last word in such arguments because I just cannot be bothered for long to bandy opposing opinions backwards and forwards. Basically I am a believer in evolution, not revolution, i.e., that you cannot forcibly persuade people to alter their opinions, they must come to such changes of their own volition. Jess, by contrast, remains a fervent and active believer in real and positive change, revolution – if needs be, since the end in her opinion justifies the means, a bloody revolution.

For such an activist, then, the current domestic scene, as it suddenly fell into place, was a daunting one. For the first time in twenty-five years of married turmoil – and, let us be thankful, a good deal of bliss – Jess now found herself at a loose end. There were a number of reasons for this, which happened unfortunately to have coincided. First, we had not long moved back to West Cornwall, a move which necessitated Jess selling up her thriving pottery business in Fowey … as a consequence, instead of working at the pottery every day, Jess had no place to go. In fact, of course, the idea had always been to set up a new pottery here at the Mill House, and I have recounted in *An Old Mill by the Stream* how

Stephen and I had got so far as converting an old former pigsty into a respectable pottery studio, fully equipped with electric wheel and large kiln, shelving bins, etc.

We were rather proud of this building, with its huge glass windows looking directly out on the bubbling stream: could anyone possibly fail to appreciate such a delightful and inspiring workshop? Well, yes – Jess. She did not, in fact, appear to want to use it at all. After a few desultory visits, once or twice rolling a few balls of clay – at Christmas, under some pressure, making for the household a much needed set of coffee mugs – she had ceased even to make the long journey from house to workshop, all of thirty feet or so. One day, after some incessant prodding from the family, she came out baldly with the final pronouncement: 'I am *not* going to start pottery again. I've finished with pottery – it's all over.'

Hence the first reason for Jess's inactivity. The second, I suppose, was the final disintegration of 'the family'. Not, I hasten to say in the wider sense of the word: Val Bakers wherever they may be, all over the wide world, remain intuitively entwined and forgather at unexpected moments from time to time ... and long may the process continue. But in the practical sense – well, yes, even I could see that 'they' were gone, all gone. Ah, sweet childhood memories! How often do I remember nostalgically those faraway family days at St. Christopher's, our big house on the edge of Porthmeor Beach where, miraculously, we had a bedroom for each child. How well I could remember, when they were all out at school, wandering round and peeping into each room, marvelling at each microscopic world so revealed – Martin's methodicalness, Gill's neatness, Jane's untidiness, Stephen's possessiveness, Demelza's security-consciousness, Genevieve's artisticness. Even now the indulgent memories make me sad – Jess, too, I fancy, though outwardly she stoically professes to be glad the birds have left the nest.

Be that as it may the result has had a disturbing effect on us both, leaving us with a great sense of sadness and loss ... in Jess's case in particular, a void in her life. Suddenly she found there was no longer anything for her to *do*; no babies to be cared for, not even a growing teenager with problems to be solved.

The third reason for Jess's lost-in-a-limbo state might be said to be the English weather. Although we both knew from our times in the area twenty years before that the weather in West Cornwall *could* be heavenly – sun in December, daffodils in January etc. – the sad fact remained that ever since we had moved back the weather had been positively beastly. Now in our second winter, the rain came pouring down, day after day, and if it wasn't raining, it was windy – great gusts of winds blowing in from the Atlantic, shivering the trees, scattering the leaves, whining in the eaves of the house. Not the sort of weather for outdoor activities – in short, not the sort of weather to encourage Jess's one genuine spare-time activity, gardening. The exciting prospects offered by the rambling gardens at the Mill House had been one of the main reasons for our choosing to come down here in the valley, where one assumed life would be reasonably protected from wind and rain, while yet open to several hours of sunlight daily.

At the beginning Jess had revelled in her new gardener's life, planting and sowing and looking forward to reaping. Alas, things had not worked out that way. Apart from the wind and rain there was the discomforting fact that we were away on our boat *Sanu* every summer just at the time when most of the crops bore fruit. What with this and the bad weather Jess became increasingly dispirited. True every now and then, rather maliciously I thought, she would browbeat me into 'helping' in the garden – which meant digging several rows of earth, uprooting trees, mowing the lawn, mundane tasks like that.

It used to get me down, for I am just not interested in gardening, and I was heartily relieved when, seeing an advertisement in the local paper Jess decided to call in a young man who went round rotavating. In a single day he had turned up more earth than I could have done in a year, but somehow Jess was not satisfied. She found fault with the rotavating, as she had found fault with the way I used a spade. Plainly she was becoming a very dissatisfied woman, than which there is no more difficult creature.

Fortunately about this time we found a temporary solution to Jess's problem. Way back in that period of her 'other life', shrouded in the mists of pre-war times, Jess had been a university student, taking a medical degree. It was a life she had very much enjoyed, and is wont to bring up regretfully at times of marital disagreements. One day, reading the newspapers with their large scale announcements, she realised that she was just the sort of 'mature student' being invited to enrol in the newly formed Open University. Excited for the first time for a long period, Jess sent in her application. Much to her relief (and mine!) she was accepted and enrolled for a one year special course studying 'The Biological Bases of Behaviour'.

Soon, rather ironically, Jess began to 'live for the post' in just the same neurotic manner with which I have been accustomed to exist for several decades. Whereas in the past she used to attack me violently for being so pathetically dependant on the post – now *she* went in search of the postman, and came bearing the day's offerings into my office in order to make sure she quickly had access to any of her letters. I must say she was seldom disappointed. Whatever else the Open University may or may not have achieved, it must have set up some sort of record for making use of the postal service. Hardly a day went by without Jess receiving some huge fat packet of instructions, counter instructions, synopses, course outlines, time tables and so forth. Now and then, too, there would be parcels: some of them, to my mind, quite astounding in their potential financial value – one set of experimental phials and materials represented about £50.

All these items were seized on joyfully by Jess who would then retire to a little home-made study she had created up in our bedroom. For me, who loves to be left alone each morning to get on with my own work, it was a halcyon period, compared to the previous few months when, bereft of aim or occupation Jess used to prowl around malevolently, sometimes breaking in on me to demand assistance with this or that horticultural chore. Now all was totally different; a great peace reigned over the Mill House as its two remaining occupants worked away at their 'lasts'.

Obviously Jess derived great stimulus from her new interest, and indeed its existence enabled me to spend a pleasant and productive winter. Very gradually, though, certain problems began to emerge, at least for an Open University student living a couple of miles from Land's End. The Open University is a fine idea, but it does mean a rather solitary existence for its students. In most cases this sense of solitude is alleviated by a system of regular group tutorials held somewhere central to each district. I imagine this works very well in Manchester or Birmingham, London or Bristol, or even in countrified but well populated districts such as Essex or Kent or Berkshire or Bucks. In Cornwall there are likely to be a few geographical problems (though for all I know they do not appertain so much in the case of more popular courses).

'The Biological Bases of Behaviour' is not what would be called a popular course, and it quickly transpired that not merely was Jess the most westerly of all the Open University students taking such a course – she was in fact one of only five in the whole of Cornwall! This meant that when she received a card summoning her to one of the periodical group get-togethers, the venue was likely to be somewhere central to the whole of Cornwall, such as St. Austell, about 60 miles from our home (involving a total journey of 120 miles) and on top of that, if she made the journey she would be seeing, assuming they were all able to make equally long and difficult journeys, a total of four other students!

Understandably this lack of fellowship did begin to depress Jess, as it depressed the only other student anywhere within reach, Madge Powell over at Portreath (and even that was 25 miles distance). At least the two of them were able to see each other fairly frequently, and confer for hours on the phone, and this helped Jess to keep on with what would otherwise have been a totally lonely task. There were also pleasant but very occasional get-togethers at Plymouth Polytechnic College, when the five Cornish students would be augmented by about twelve from various parts of South Devon.

Far more rewarding, Jess found was the final summertime week's refresher course, held at the University of Sussex near Brighton. Attending it meant that Jess had to miss a part of her annual holiday on *Sanu*, but she did not regret this when she measured against it the excitement of really feeling back in university, caught up in a feverish week's activity along with not five or twenty-five but two-hundred fellow students, people from all walks of life, young and old, thin and fat, all kinds.

For one week she sank right back into the atmosphere of university life, for lectures are held in the university class rooms and there are meals in the university cafeteria, and late night sessions in the university bar ... All this under the tutorial direction of several brilliant teachers of psychology including the (to Jess) legendary Stephen Rose, author of several best selling books. No wonder that when she finally joined us after her week her eyes were sparkling and her head buzzing with new ideas.

After all this it must have seemed something of a let-down to be back at the Mill House for a third winter with the one year course finished, and nothing to look forward to but the news as to whether or not she had passed her final examination. In the end the news came, and Jess had passed: and then – slump-down again.

It was at this moment of 'low' that Jess hit on a new idea. She did not particularly want to carry on with the Open University since she found the working in a limbo – which living in Cornwall involved – rather depressing, and it was likely to be even more so on a three year course, the next natural step. Besides, the one week refresher courses did interfere with *Sanu* trips. However, there *was* another approach altogether: and that was to think in terms of going to a normal university.

At first this seemed such a revolutionary idea that even Jess was a little diffident.

'Of course I don't suppose I'd get accepted. I mean – I *am* old.'

It was true that fifty seemed a little old for a university

student. But then I remembered some years previously a friend of ours, the wife of a fellow CND member at Exeter, had actually gone back to university when well into her fifties – and was now, we heard, a teacher. Gradually, as we began looking into things in more depth, we found that the concept of mature students at university was a good deal more than idle talk. Most universities, it seemed, were prepared to consider them – many actually accepted a small quota each year.

Thus encouraged Jess sat down and wrote off for the booklet put out by the Universities Examinations Board which outlines a list of British Universities and their subjects. Back came a huge tome full of fascinating information about the forty or so universities which specialised in psychology, the subject Jess had decided she wanted to study. These universities (about two thirds of the total) ranged from Edinburgh in the far north to Exeter in the South West.

We had a stimulating and rather sobering morning browsing through the book and trying to pick out the most likely universities. After all (as I was beginning to realise in some dismay) the consequence of what we were so light heartedly doing now might well become quite momentous.

Although I felt it only fair to encourage Jess in her new interest, could see the logic of her argument that now at long last she was free to do something with her own life – nevertheless I was bound to recognise, probably too late, that such a development might well profoundly alter our way of life. At the very least it would mean being away from Cornwall for large periods of each year, and if economics necessitated letting our house in order to finance the project – well, then we might be away for as long as three years.

Of course there were alternatives!

'I've got the perfect solution,' said Jess. 'I'll go and live with one of my sisters, that'll save renting anywhere – and *you* can stay down here and keep an eye on the donkeys.'

At the time I chose to ignore such remarks or to assume them to be humorous: but sometimes I couldn't help wondering! However, of one thing I was sure: for Jess to go and stay with one of her sisters was a fatal idea – like many families they had drifted far apart over the years, and it was easy to imagine the old friction which would develop.

At first we made out a list of six possible universities, to each of which Jess wrote an official letter. The answers as they came were rather illuminating. One in Scotland, alas, made it pretty clear that they didn't want to be bothered with a mature student – and anyway why didn't she try an English university? Others, like Bangor and London and Exeter, were all most friendly and suggested that they would be happy to consider Jess's formal applications. One university actually provisionally offered acceptance then and there, provided Jess satisfied the usual requirements of entry. This was, of all places, Liverpool – home of one of the sisters!

'There!' said Jess triumphantly.

'Liverpool!' I said with great feeling. 'You can't seriously want to move from Cornwall to *Liverpool*.'

This was no idle slur on a great capital city on my part. I grew up in Blundellsands, a suburb of Liverpool, and – even allowing for the excitement of it being a great port, and no doubt of being the birthplace of the Beatles – I can't but remember it as a place of considerable desolation, convenient only as a stepping stone to the beauty spots of North Wales.

'Not Liverpool!'

Jess decided not to pursue that possibility for the moment, and we became harmoniously joined again in considering what seemed to us the most attractive venue, Bangor in North Wales. Here again I have to declare a personal interest, for my family all come from Llanfairfechan, near Bangor, I spent all my possible childhood and teenage holidays in the area, wrote my first novel with it as a setting, and retain all the natural romantic conceptions one associates with happy childhood times. So, selfishly, if Jess had to go to university somewhere and I was to be with her, I rather hoped the chosen place might be Bangor, surrounded as it is by all the beauties of Snowdonia, the picturesque island life of Anglesey, and the childhood remembered delights of Llanfairfechan, Conway and Llandudno.

'I do think, you know,' I said casually, at the end of a long morning. 'Bangor sounds about the most interesting.'

All these preparations for Jess's future mature education were, of course, long term ones, relating to a year or two ahead, even assuming she got accepted somewhere. In the meantime more immediate life had to go on, and we were finding finances difficult now that Jess had stopped earning. Hopefully we evolved a new pattern of searching through the *Western Morning News* every day for potential jobs which Jess could apply.

Surprisingly there were quite a few: two in particular appealed to her, one as an administrator for the Cornwall Naturalist Trust, the other as a traveller in Cornwall for a well known firm of publishers. The latter remained a mystery as we never heard another word, but for the former Jess was obviously a potentially suitable candidate. They wanted a retired person on a part time basis, preferably with a special interest in nature – and Jess fitted all the requirements. It sounded a fascinating job, for the Trust was very active at the time in Cornwall, helping to protect specific areas from the encroachment of property speculators and so forth. Yes, it sounded interesting, and Jess waited eagerly for her interview ...

Perhaps we should have consulted Jess's stars, for all at once her life took an urgent tangent. For some years she had been told by her doctor that at some future date she would need to have a remedial operation for prolapse of the womb, a common complaint among women of her age. Now suddenly she received word to attend Redruth Hospital for the operation.

At first Jess hesitated. As a child she had spent long periods in hospital, especially after a car accident had broken her legs, and even in the early years of marriage she seemed continually in and out of hospital. Consequently she had grown to value the very long period of twenty years since she had been a patient. Now, voluntarily, to put herself into those once familiar surroundings seemed tempting fate.

Finally however, persuaded that it would be for the best in

the long run, in she went. I drove her over one wintry afternoon and left her at the sister's room, looking quite bright and cheerful, and went home to a suddenly lonely Mill House – back to a world of donkeys and dogs and cats and swaying trees and rushing water.

The next morning the operation was carried out, and that evening I called at the hospital – to find, to my dismay, that Jess was still under sedation but obviously in rather bad shape. The operation had been successful but obviously more serious than we had been led to suppose.

The next three weeks proved something of a small nightmare. Owing to unexpected complications Jess was a very long time recovering from what we had assumed was a purely routine operation. She suffered great discomfort and pain, and altogether, understandably, grew extremely depressed. One of the things that saved her sanity, I think, was the company of several other women who had been through much the same experiences. They were mostly local Cornish women, people she had never met before, all of whom she found kind and warmhearted. The nurses, too, were very sweet, and Jess could not have wished for better treatment. It was just that everything seemed to take so long.

At times like this one is grateful for the friends who show their friendship in action. Of course Genevieve and Martin, our two children who happened to be still in Cornwall, came over frequently – Genny was then still a student at nearby Redruth Art School, and able to pop in every lunchtime and sit and chat. Other friends from further afield came over on the afternoon visits – Jack and Pat Richards, little Jackie Durrant, our potter friend, Anthony and Christianne, Judith and Peter from Polruan. I was very grateful to see them, as I am sure Jess was – on her their welcome smiling faces acted as a real tonic.

From way up in the Midlands two of our oldest friends, Frank and Kate Baker wrote that they were planning to come down for a long weekend and would visit Jess. As it happened, Jess started really recovering and I was able to collect her from hospital a day or two before Frank and Kate's journey down –

so that in the end they came over to see us at the Mill House, instead of hospital.

I was very glad of their visit, not only because Jess, still very weak and wan, was greatly cheered by such company, but because they brought with them their own great friend, the Royal Shakespeare Company actor Richard Pasco, with whom I had corresponded ever since enthusiastically he became a subscriber to the *Cornish Review*. By a strange coincidence I had always remembered seeing Richard Pasco in almost the very first performance of John Osborne's *Look Back in Anger* at the Royal Court Theatre all of twenty years or more previously. It was nice to be able to tell him, even after all this time, how much I'd admired that performance.

As his name might suggest, Richard was Cornish, or certainly half Cornish. He was one of that rather attractive breed of exiles who are forever paying fleeting visits to their romantic home and bringing with them such waves of enthusiasm that it somehow renews your own attachment. Jess and I liked him very much – especially when he made a fuss of our two donkeys, standing stoically in their field, glad to see visitors.

Luke-warm as my own attitude to the donkeys had always been I had to admit to myself that they might be the therapeutic weapon in aiding Jess's convalescence. So, much against my real inclinations, I allowed myself to be persuaded into taking them out for daily walks with myself holding Esmeralda's bridle, Jess riding on her back, and Lulu, the impish baby, trotting behind.

'Just one thing – I don't want anyone to see me like this. We'll go up Gilly Lane, take the back route, it's completely deserted, never see anyone along there.'

Gilly Lane really was a deserted area, so much so that grass grew in the middle of the road. I felt pretty safe in choosing such a secluded route, safe from prying eyes. Even without external problems, however, the journey was a difficult one, for we had acquired an extra companion, a noisy and disobedient puppy, Roxy.

We presented, I realised, a somewhat eccentric picture –

first myself, windblown and wild, striding out in front, my hand firmly grasping the bridle of a somewhat unwilling Esmeralda, who plodded along rather miserably at about one mile an hour, trying every now and then to stop to nibble at the passing hedge ... on her back, enfolded in various protective robes against a brisk wind, Jess looking like some proverbial matriarch of old ... following behind, or perhaps I should say frisking behind, the sloe-eye Lulo, attached by a very long rope to Esmeralda, not above periodically stopping and digging in her heels and bringing the whole procession to a stop ... and finally now, Roxy, who ran forward and backwards and under the donkeys' feet and generally caused turmoil. Still, at least we had the whole quiet country lane to ourselves, we could spread out comfortably –

'Honk! Honk!'

Astonishingly, a car was approaching. Desperately I pulled Esmeralda into the hedge – perversely Lulu wandered over to the other side of the lane. Excited by the noise of a car Roxy started running round and round barking furiously.

Ahead a large saloon car pulled obediently to a stop, unable to progress further because of Lulu's rope stretched across the lane. Four or five people peered out enthusiastically.

'Oooooh! Look at the darling donkeys – aren't they *lovely*.'

And so on.

I blushed crimson and somehow dragged Lulu to the other side of the road. With some difficulty – as Roxy kept jumping up trying to lick the occupants' faces – the car started up and drove on.

Swearing I dragged at Esmeralda's bridle and tugged her back into the road, and we resumed our journey.

A moment later – Honk! Honk! – and another car swept round the corner out of nowhere, and we went through the same pantomime.

When the same thing happened in quick succession a third and fourth time I realised that something out of the ordinary must be happening. It was. One of the local hunts was out that afternoon and had chosen to take a route along the back roads. Gilly Lane was being used by the hunt followers, a seemingly endless stream of cars, over twenty in all which now came along one after another. That wasn't all, either. Soon huntmen on horses came riding along, at once the subject of fierce barking and pretended attacks by a completely uncontrolled Roxy. One or two of the horses reared up, the huntsmen shouted, Roxy barked, I swore. Only Jess, sitting serenely content on the top of Esmeralda seemed to enjoy the humour of the situation . . . At the end of it all, when finally and wearily I dragged the beasts of burden home, at least Jess looked pink and flushed and happy – indeed, as she said, quite rejuvenated.

IV
Old Cars Forever

That winter was to prove notable for other problems besides those of wife and water ... there was, for instance, the increasingly urgent matter of 'the cars'. All my life I have been a lover and user of old cars. Even as I write these words my mind immediately switches back to a dear little Austin Seven in which, more than twenty-five years ago I first ventured upon Cornish roads. It was a gay little car, which I painted a bright blue and white, with a map of Cornwall drawn on one side, and across it printed the bold words *The Cornish Review*, to advertise my newest baby.

Almost at the same time that I launched the *Review* I had married Jess, and when we arrived back in Cornwall from London, there was my familiar little Austin waiting for us at the station. Jess was not, I think, greatly impressed, for in those days old cars literally had a look of having been held together by pieces of string. When I proceeded to stick her into a tiny seat and then drive her at great speed up into the hills around Trencrom, for her first visit to my little cottage there – well I think she liked the car even less.

In fact, that small Austin was merely the first of a whole series of old cars which passed through our family. Many of these I purchased from Jack Collinson, an eccentric car dealer who kept a small museum of old cars at the small village of Angarrack, near Hayle ... among them a two seater Austin 6 with a dicky, a four seater Austin 12 with a bright red head (the joy and delight of our children) and one of my own particular favourites, a rakish old Rover 12, the sort with an enormous long bonnet and over drive and many other refinements. In these and similar old monstrosities Jess and I, with our gathering brood, used to whizz happily around the Cornish lanes, never driving very fast, but probably getting a great deal more pleasure out of our vehicles than most people.

Undoubtedly the pride and joy of that period, the *pièce de résistance*, was an old London taxi which we bought on impulse, for £50, while holidaying in London, early in our marriage. In those days the big London taxi cab company used to keep a row of used taxis in their Brixton garage and sell them off to devotees like myself. For a long time I think we were the only London taxi running around Cornwall. Later on Mary John, married to Augustus John's son and living in the fishing port of Mousehole, bought one – it was always a great moment when the two of us met and honked our old fashioned horns! In those days we lived at the old vicarage at St. Hilary, some five miles outside Penzance, and our old taxi was endlessly useful – for taking the family shopping on Saturday mornings, for carting around loads of pottery, even for a time as a lorry for supplying bags of firewood from house to house! Another extremely useful function of the taxi was to serve as a Saturday mid-day resting house for all our children: we used to buy them large packets of fish and chips and leave them to guzzle while we all enjoyed a mid day drink in St. John's House pub! Another rather special occasion with the taxi that comes to mind is when we all entered the Newlyn Carnival, and the old taxi was dolled up with bright flags and streamers, and bedecked with beautiful girls (we won the first prize, too, for a take-off of the Kon Tiki Raft Expedition).

Yes, I have loved thee, old cars, in my fashion most of my life ... Now, at the Mill House, rather regrettably, I discovered that my sons Stephen and Martin were following in my motoring footsteps. Stephen began the trend by acquiring for £30 an incredibly dilapidated but apparently functional Austin 30 van. Decrepit it might be to look at but at least it provided Stephen with mobility and for a few weeks he was happy buzzing around West Cornwall in his new toy, calling on all his old friends. Often too, the return of the little green van would mean that Stephen's old friends had been brought back for a get-together, an event which did not always bring joy to our aged hearts, for we value our sleep. Still, as long as Stephen's car functioned it meant he was independent and mobile, and there would be less likelihood of his infuriating old habit of wanting to borrow my car.

Alas, suddenly Stephen's van fell ill – indeed, very speedily, went into a rapid decay. It first broke down somewhere on the road to Penzance, and after various expeditions to try and get it working, I was prevailed on to go out with a tow rope and bring Stephen back home. Before long I was to regret this wanton gesture, as day after day the weary old van sat in the middle of our drive, lifeless and forlorn. Sometimes Stephen would spend several hours working away in the bowels of the engine, but nothing he did would seem to bring life back.

'It's no good,' he said despairingly, 'It's kaput – finished.'

This was not exactly the end of Stephen's van, alas. Four of us got behind it and somehow manhandled it into a space beside my office. True I had rather been intending to try and turn that space into a proper garage – no matter, at least it wasn't the drive. In the middle of that space we deposited Stephen's van, R.I.P.

A week later, perhaps by now constitutionally unable to live without a car, Stephen informed us he had invited his friend Alvin to live with him. What he really meant, of course, was that he had invited Alvin's *Mini* to live with him! So now, day by day, the little bright blue Mini stood in our drive, and Jess and I often looked out with some disapproval.

'All I want to see when I look out of the window,' said Jess crossly, 'are trees and shrubs and birds and bees ... Not Alvin's Mini.'

I knew only too well what Jess meant, as already we had been through big scenes about our own car; or rather, unfortunately, *cars*. When we moved down to the Mill House we had a useful old blue Austin Cambridge which served our modest purposes admirably. Unfortunately on one of our trips out to our boat *Sanu*, at Agde on the South of France, we had

had to leave the car there for some months, until Stephen was able to bring it back … in the meantime, carless, we had found life deep in the country impossible. As usual in such matters, I had telephoned Jack Collinson.

'Do you happen to have a reliable old car going cheap?'

'Yes, one you might like – come and see for yourself.'

It was waiting for me when I got there – *another* old Austin Cambridge, this time painted a dull grey, but serviceable enough by the look of it. Since Jack was selling it off for the incredible sum of £37.50, I did not bandy words but wrote out a cheque – and drove home. It wasn't until I got home that I really studied the log book and then discovered that by a strange coincidence the car had originally belonged to someone at Porthcurno, about two miles from our own home!

At any rate the grey Austin Cambridge had saved our peace of mind … and then in the process of time, Stephen brought home the blue one, and there were two quite large Austin Cambridges standing in the drive. Until, as I was saying, Jess had made her displeasure known. That was when I had to get a scythe and cut a large patch out of the shrubs opposite my office until I had made space enough for parking our two Austin Cambridges. It was not at all a convenient business, often involving several runs and re-runs, so that already, you might say, car life at the Mill House was a little congested.

And now Alvin's Mini was there to stir things up.

'It'll have to be moved,' decreed Jess. 'I want my view.'

For a time the Mini was hounded from pillar to post; one day it would be tucked in some incredible corner of the garden, another almost inside my office – perhaps another time outside the front gate. To us it always seemed an unhappy sort of car. After a time we gathered that it was *very* unhappy, the big end was going, and Alvin went about with a worried expression.

'Perhaps you ought to sell it?' we said hopefully.

Then one day Stephen and Alvin returned in great glee. They had had a real stroke of luck. A friend of theirs had been going to put his old Mini on the scrap heap – so they had bought it instead.

'Marvellous for spare parts, you see.'

'*Where* is it?' we said apprehensively.

'Oh, that's all right,' Stephen explained smoothly, 'We won't bring it actually into the grounds – we'll keep it out in the lane.'

That was precisely what they did. The old broken down black Mini was parked permanently by our front gate, creating endless hazards – and Alvin's original, though currently defunct Mini, remained where it was – more or less in our drive.

'Don't worry,' said Stephen. 'Alvin's very good mechanically – he's going to swop engines. You'll see – we'll have a super Mini at the end of it all.'

In the midst of all this, like some dark omen of further car doom, there arrived our other son, Martin – in *his* old Austin Cambridge. Unlike our two elder Austin Cambridges, or indeed any of the other cars around, Martin's car, at least initially, was a joy to behold; very clean, without rust, in first class condition. But ... well it had to be parked somewhere. And in the end it started to lie around – in our drive.

'Can you believe it?' said Jess one day incredulously, looking out of the window. 'I ask you, can you believe it?'

Martin's part in the saga was not finished. When the time came for his car to take the Test, although far and away the most impressive of our cars – it failed. Desolate Martin scanned the advertisements in the local paper and (unfortunately as it happened) managed to find another Austin Cambridge advertised for £50. Ignoring our wise warnings he rushed off and bought the car, arriving back later that day face bright with hopeful smiles, at the wheel of a very grand old Austin Cambridge indeed. Possibly this looked even smarter than his previous one – undoubtedly, alas, it proved to be in poorer condition. Week after week something different went wrong with Martin's latest acquisition so that he was constantly paying out more and more money.

At last, after numerous upsets and breakdowns, from which often Martin would arrive home by bus completely exhausted late at night, the time came for the second Austin Cambridge to take its Test. And ... yes, you've guessed it ..., that failed too.

And so, to our own two Austin Cambridges, there were now added Martin's permanent monuments, *his* two Austin Cambridges.

'As I was saying,' Jess remarked one day in absolute despair, 'It's quite, *quite*, unbelievable.'

I must admit she had considerable excuse for her exasperation. Sometimes when I came walking back from Tresidder with our milk, as I came over the hump before the lane led down to the Mill House I saw what looked like the site of a garage there ahead of me. By rights the vista should have been of a long line of elm trees, a lawn, and beyond it the familiar grey granite shape of the Mill House. In fact what the eye saw was – cars, cars and more cars – a green van, a couple of bright Minis, and four Austin Cambridges. And of course, should anyone be misguided enough to call on us by car – well they would be hard put to find a parking space.

Still, when all is said and done, you do need a car in the country! It would be difficult to imagine how we would exist, let alone enjoy life without a car at the Mill House. The nearest bus is a mile away, and the service pretty dismal. Although we do a lot of walking locally, our car gives us that much wider choice. If we want a change from Land's End, we can quickly nip along the coast road through the mining villages of St. Just and Pendeen, out to the marvellous moors around Zennor and Gurnard's Head – or perhaps down to the strange haunted world of Botallack, mine shafts roaring against the sky like forlorn memorials. In our car we have the entry to Godrevy, to Hell's Mouth, to Looe Pool, to Gunwalloe, to Kynance Cove and the Lizard – to Falmouth and Myler and Flushing – to many a pleasant day's outing.

One trip that we made around this time was like going back in time, across to Hayle Towans. When we used to live in a cottage on Trencrom Hill we often took the children down to the deserted beach below Lelant. I suppose most people think of Cornwall as a wild rugged place, a panorama of fierce jagged rocks and towering cliffs, majestic hills. So it can be, of course. But sometimes here and there, scattered around the coastline, you may sometimes come across a different sort of landscape. Instead of rocks, a wide sweep of sands: instead of high cliffs a low array of squashed sand dunes stretching back inland.

Such a place is Hayle Towans, whose dunes often seem to be placed like sentinels designed hopefully but inadequately to block the advance of moving sand and sea. Every now and then a gale blews ... when the wind has subsided the thin grass reeds on top of the dunes look even more lonely, the massive slopes of sand have pushed a little further inland. Looking over the expanse it is easy to envisage the sand swallowing up not only the humps but the fields and the houses and the people behind – and perhaps afterwards the sea flooding forward in some final deluge.

I have always been fascinated by the Hayle Estuary, which of course we got to know much better some years after Trencrom when we decided to keep our old boat *Sanu* there. Once Hayle had been a busy port but the existence of a sand bar across the entrance had been partly responsible for a decline in trade. There was still a regular traffic of coal and scrap boats which came in on one tide and usually left on the next after unloading. Most of these large boats followed the narrow channel that wound up past the big electricity works and into the town of Hayle itself, where there were commercial wharves. However about a couple of hundred yards inside the sand bar there was a fork in the river, and the narrow right hand channel led up to an old disused quay known as Lelant Quay. Like St. Ive's harbour this quay dried out at low tide but the bottom was reasonably flat, with a mixture of shingle and sand, and there was room alongside for several large boats.

Here we kept *Sanu* for a couple of winters, leaning against the quay, her huge fat bottom daily exposed for inspection. We used to come down two or three times a week, especially on the weekends, and spend many pleasant hours working on the boat, some of the time relaxing sitting on the deck and surveying the always changing views. There is something

quite weird, even ghostly about the whole setting of the Hayle
Estuary, ranging from the quite wide shallow bird sanctuary
pool lining the main road, out to the narrow inlet which snakes
in across the bar. This sense of strange desolation continues
across to the Towans. Some flavour of it all was captured for
me very vividly by an old friend Erma Harvey James, an
embroideress and puppeteer, who spent her childhood at
Hayle:

> I always used to find the vast stretch of sea and shore
> indescribably melancholy. And the miles of sand dunes
> stretching as far as the red river of Gwithian which
> stained the sea crimson as though some monstrous
> creature had perished upstream in a torrent of blood.
> Perhaps it was simply that it was all too dream-like,
> verging on another reality ... There was a tradition that
> the Towans had once all been meadowland and that the
> sand covered it in a single night. Marram grass and sea
> couch grass had been planted to stabilise the shifting
> dunes, but there were still 'open' ones with shifting sand.
> Among the dunes were the remains of the old Dynamite
> Works where one day during the war an explosion had
> occurred which sent everyone within miles running in
> panic from their houses and had broken the windows of
> the church of St. Ives on the other side of the bay. There
> was scarcely a family in Hayle who had not lost someone
> on that dreadful morning. Some of the ruins still stood
> among the languid waving grasses. And in a wild garden
> of bugles and sea holly doorways opened on to a void and
> flights of granite steps led up into the empty air ...

The whole Hayle area, in fact, like so many of the less
immediately touristy parts of Cornwall, is full of strange
fascination. Down back streets of the town, one comes across
stately Georgian houses, some of them quite large, which were
once the homes of wealthy merchants of the eighteenth
century. Not long ago we were shown round one of these that
used to belong to a member of the Harvey family, who

developed Hayle as a port: the house still had a faded elegance, every room seemed to have superb proportions, everywhere space and relaxation ... Perhaps as a sign of the times the house has now become the centre for a bird sanctuary where a couple from London, Mike Reynolds and his wife, have set up a really fascinating collection of exotic foreign birds, visited by more than 50,000 people a year.

There are many half-known places like Hayle which are well worth exploring in Cornwall, and in fact – thanks to a car! – we have done a good deal of exploring ourselves. We were originally encouraged along this way in the days when we ran our own studio pottery and would deliver pots to quite remote shops in all corners of our favourite county – to places like Polzeath on the north coast, a barren and deserted stretch of sands in the winter – a popular surfing beach in the summer. When deserted we would wander along the flat sands listening to the booming waves and being aware of some sort of timelessness ... alas at the height of the summer season Polzeath suffered considerably. It was put very well by John Betjeman, who used to holiday regularly there, in a poem he wrote for our *Cornish Review*:

> Now as we near the ocean roar,
> A smell of deep-fry haunts the shore.
> In pools beyond the reach of tide
> The Senior Service cartons glide
> And on the sand the surf line lisps
> With wrappings of potato crisps.
> The breakers bring with merry noise
> Tribute of broken plastic toys
> And lichened spears of blackthorn glitter
> With harvest of the August litter.
> Here in the late October light
> See Cornwall, a pathetic sight,
> Raddled and put upon and tired
> And looking somewhat ever-hired,
> Remembering in the autumn air
> The years when she was young and fair –

Those golden and unpeopled bays,
The shadowy cliffs and sheep worn ways,
The legions of unsurfed on surf,
The thyme and mushroom scented turf.
The slate hung farms, the oil lit chapels,
Thin elms and lemon coloured apples –
Going and gone beyond recall
Now she is free for One and All.
One day a tidal wave will break
Before the breakfasters awake
And sweep the carns out to sea
The oil the tar and you and me
And leave in windy criss-cross motion
A waste of undulating ocean
From which jut out, a second Scilly,
The Isles of Roughtor and Brown Willy.

I always enjoy the pithy way our Poet Laureate writes about Cornwall; often in a deft phrase he seems to capture the endless paradox which haunts this marvellous county. On the one hand it is so strange and mysterious and beautiful that one wants everyone to see and enjoy it – on the other hand *if* everyone follows that advice the very mystery and magic is swamped by the invasion of thousands and thousands of cars and caravans and endless streams of tourists.

There is no easy answer to this problem, but perhaps fortunately for those of us who live in Cornwall, the winter months offer a chance of respite ... and it is then, as I was saying earlier, that we used to make our explorations. If anyone wants to enjoy some of our own surprises – then visit such spots as Portloe, on the Roseland peninsula, or St. Just in Roseland: Manaccan or Gorran on the Lizard or on the other side little fishing villages like Cadgwith; or an old fishing port like Porthleven, with its adjoining unusual beauty spot, the mysterious Looe Pool, an inland lake right on the edge of the sea, and joined by an underground tunnel. Or up on the north coast, apart from Polzeath, visit my one time home of Portquin, or nearby Port Isaac where the fishing boats are still drawn up the pebble beach – or such wild spots, unbearable in the summer, grandly desolate in winter, as Widemouth Bay or Bedruthan Steps, along the popular road to Newquay. Even Newquay itself, forever doomed to be the 'Blackpool' of summertime Cornwall, acquires a certain brooding desolation in the winter to ameliorate its pervasive view of hideous modern bungalows and endless garish guest houses.

Yes, Jess and I used to enjoy our forays around Cornwall, for almost every new expedition seemed to bring some unexpected reward. Certainly it gave me not only food for thought, but material for my books. I find that out of a total of thirty books which I have now had published, during a writing career of just over thirty years, at least half of them have had some direct connection with my adopted county. Like many another creative worker – painters, sculptors, potters as well as writers – I have found Cornwall a seemingly endless source of inspiration. Sometimes it has been enough to glance out of a railway carriage and see a passing Cornish scene – the result a complete short story, perhaps a whole novel. It is not something I can explain at all, any more than I expect can a painter.

One or two examples have always stuck firmly in my memory. It was indeed looking out of a railway carriage that gave me the idea for a successful short story, 'The Woman and the Engine Driver' – through seeing an attractive but rather sad-looking housewife leaning over the garden gate of a remote country cottage.

On another occasion I was taken by some friends to an isolated country club near Helston where the clientele appeared to consist mainly of flying officers from a nearby airfield – the atmosphere was so strange (an old fashioned gramophone was playing 1940s' jazz tunes) that immediately the idea came to me: supposing this was all unreal, a ghost scene – afterwards we found the place did not exist? This was the basis of a broadcast story, 'The Anniversary'. Another much published story, 'The Sacrifice', or 'Death at the Carn' as it has sometimes been called, was the direct result of a wander over Zennor moors to an old carn – up in those weird surroundings it was easy to project one back into the ritualistic times of the druids of old. Two of my own favourite stories, 'The Flameswallower' and 'The Clay Pool', derived from moments in time – standing at Corpus Christi Fair, Penzance and watching a flameswallower in action, and being all alone by the blue quarry pool up above Nancledra, and imbibing its weird vibrations. It is not necessary, in my experience, to have any kind of lengthy revelation, far from it – perhaps the most ambitious, and certainly the longest story I have ever written about Cornwall, 'A Pebble on the Beach', recently issued in a collection, *A Summer to Remember*, was derived in all its 20,000 words from picking up and feeling between my fingers a single small white pebble . . .

In general I have found it wiser to confine such writings to the short story, for of course the inspiration does not always translate successfully into the final form. Once or twice I have wasted months of my working life by too hurriedly attempting to turn a momentary inspiration into a full length novel. In my early days in Cornwall, for instance, I was constantly intrigued by the weird Hayle estuary setting of which I have now been writing, and conceived what seemed to me a fascinating novel about a strange family living in a cafe on the water's edge, with many macabre happenings. In a fury I wrote the whole novel, but something went wrong en route and it was never published, and has now been lost forever in one of our moves.

Writing about Cornwall on non-fictional lines is at once easier – and, paradoxically, harder! What I mean is that here one has the opportunity to be much more precise, to try and convey in fine details just what sort of impression a certain place or landscape may have made upon you ... only to find, in capturing the detail, such accuracy is even harder work than the fictional approach! I knew, for example, that I have many times tried to capture the feeling of the Land's End area, indeed, have written many pages on the subject in various autobiographical books – yet I have never felt that I have captured the secret as well as did the octogenarian writer Ruth Manning Sanders in a memorable description of a walk along the cliffs at Land's End: 'It is then that the drowned sailors of the past can be heard hailing their names above the moaning of the waters. It is then that the sense of the primordial, the strange and the savage, the unknown, the very long ago, fills the dusk with something that is akin to dread. It is then that the place becomes haunted: a giant heaves grey limbs from his granite bed, a witch sits in that stone stair on the cliff.'

Perhaps too much has been written about Cornwall! I found myself thinking on these lines during the winter when at long last, after a series of cliffhanging exercises of which I have written in *Spring at Land's End*, my long beloved *Cornish Review* came to its final end. Always in the past I had felt impelled to fight for the life of this, if you like my seventh child: after all it had been founded as long ago at 1949, possibly not long after the birth of many of the young officers and committee members at the South West Arts Association who had decided, in their wisdom, to end our annual grant. Now, suddenly and strangely, I did not feel like fighting any longer. It seemed to me that although the loss of our SWAA and Cornwall County Councils were the direct causes of ending publication, the indirect, and perhaps even more decisive causes, were the almost total lack of support from among the Cornish. Typically, after the magazine had ceased, the local papers were full of sad letters, many of them from Cornish people, bemoaning the loss. My own feeling now is that the *Cornish Review* had a good long run, and its successes and failures are at least forever captured in print: upon many a bookshelf the long row of nearly forty issues will stand as irrevocable evidence of something that did exist, and did do something to portray Cornwall in all its mystery and splendour.

As a last loving task before closing the *Cornish Review* file forever, I busied myself in those winter months by making a selection from all the material we had published during a period of a quarter of a century. Apart from the fact that I found it personally absorbing to re-read all those earlier numbers, I marvelled at some of the superb pieces of writing I resurrected. Articles like R. Glynn Gryll's memorable, *Who Are The Cornish?*, Jack Clemo's *My Life in the Clay World*, Frank Baker's *The Frenzied Forties at Mevagissey*, Ida Procter's *Virginia Woolf's Cornwall*, Noel Welch's *The Du Mauriers*, Jack Pender's *Grandpa Was a Painter*, Bernard Leach's *My World as a Potter*, James Whetter's *Cornwall into the 20th Century* ... stories by Lady Vyvyan, Ronald Duncan, Daphne Du Maurier, Winston Graham, Frank Baines, David Watmough ... poems by W.S. Graham, Charles Causley, D.M. Thomas, A.L. Rowse, John Betjeman, Arthur Caddick, Zofia Ilinska, David Stringer, Frances Bellerby and, of course, Jack Clemo ... and vivid illustrations by Bryan Pearce, Alfred Wallis, Ben Nicholson, Peter Lanyon, Barbara Hepworth, Mary Jewells, Misome Piele, Jack Pender, Denis Mitchell, John Milne and Margo Maeckleberghe. Someday, I hope, this anthology of all that was best in the *Cornish Review* will see the light of day and perhaps present the final, the ultimate in penetrating revelations about Cornwall. Yes, indeed, I would like to think so. Or perhaps the task that seems beyond a single writer is equally just beyond a hundred? Perhaps Cornwall will remain forever, as I once described it, a place of eternal mystery and magic – the timeless land.

V

Here Today, Gone Tomorrow

In the New Year life seemed to begin again. Not surprisingly our thoughts turned longingly to the future: to summer and what had now become our annual family cruise on our old boat, *Sanu*. This event remained a long time away, of course, but with cruising I have learned that it is never too soon to start your preparations. I used to follow this practical axiom even in those amateur days when we first had the boat. I would often spend several anxious days working out in precise detail the navigational requirements of a trip from Falmouth to Mevagissey or Fowey, or perhaps, greatly daring to Penzance and Newlyn.

This latter trip involved a passage round the Lizard Lighthouse, that famous beacon which represents for many ocean travellers their first sight of England's green and pleasant land, and we knew from practical experience, few coastlines are more awesome or savage looking, with numerous outcrops of wicked looking rocks (to this day, for reasons beyond me, still unmarked by buoys). Oh yes, early on in our boating career I developed the healthiest of respects for the Boy Scout motto of 'Be Prepared'.

So now, in those long winter evenings, I spent many pleasurable hours pouring over my charts for our next summer cruise. First, of course, we had to decide *where* to go. During several previous summers we had busied ourselves first with taking *Sanu* out from England to the Mediterranean – then exploring the coastlines of Southern France, Elba,

Corsica, Sardinia, Italy – ending up at the latest of several winter-time 'homes', this time the George Cross island of Malta. One of our reasons for choosing Malta, apart from the very real practical advantage of being among English speaking people, was that by its very position the island made a marvellous central base for future voyages. From Malta we could if we wished travel due west towards the Balearic Isles of Majorca or Ibiza – or we could cross to the African coast, heading for Algeria or Libya or Egypt: we could return to Italy and France, with all their ceaseless attractions ... or we could take another turning, and head for the golden world of the Greek Isles.

Greece has always been our ultimate aim in the Mediterranean ever since we listened entranced to the adventurous stories of friends who have travelled out there, and so we decided that this summer Greece it should be. I took a long thoughtful look at our large map of the whole of the west Mediterranean area and worked out a sensible circuitous route. We could travel up via Syracuse and the toe of Italy and then across to Corfu, our first Greek island. After that we would laze our way through the Ionian Isles (Corfu, Paxos, Ithaca, Levkas etc), then through the gulf of Patras and into the famous Corinth Canal, that narrow $3\frac{1}{4}$ mile stretch which would bring us directly to Athens, or rather its port of Piraeus. From there we could embark on a circumnavigation of the Cyclades Isles, set like jewels in the middle of the Aegean Sea – lastly making a 400 mile leap back to Malta.

It sounded a marvellous programme, and eagerly I made a list of the necessary large scale charts and sent off for them, about thirty in all. I love the moment when these bigger charts arrive and I spread them out on my chart table: then, indeed, it really seems as if the trip has begun, as carefully I start measuring out my courses and distances, from port to port. Of course, other sources of information are necessary: the appropriate *Admiralty Pilot* (in this case Volume III and IV of the Mediterranean Pilots), together with corrections up to date – and then several of the many helpful guide books on Greece and the Greek Isles.

I was particularly lucky to have the guidance of an old (book) friend Captain Henry Denham, who has spent the past twenty years cruising around various parts of the Mediterranean and then producing A-Z navigational guides to each area: now I ordered both his *The Aegean Sea*, and a new one, *The Ionian Isles to Rhodes*. I also picked up a useful little book by another yachtsman, Ernle Bradford, entitled quite simply *The Greek Isles* – although not so practical as Denham's this was quite a literary feast, full of perfectly shaped phrases which, later on, we were to find, brought beautifully alive some remote island or anchorage.

Armed with this plentiful ammunition, I must have spent a good month early in the New Year mapping out what was really quite an ambitious cruise, involving a total distance of nearly 1,500 miles, with calls at about thirty different ports and anchorages, ranging from Piraeus a city of 500,000 people, with its huge modern marina, to tiny little islands like the potters' home, Siphnos, or Ios or Kea or Seriphos ... not forgetting Santorini, our ultimate aim, the famed volcanic island which many scholars regarded as the original Atlantis.

Oh, yes, we were going to have a stupendous cruise this summer, with visits to Epidaurus, Greece's national open air theatre which seats 14,000 people and where, so they said, you could hear a pin drop on the stage from the highest point ... to Delphi, home of the oracles, perhaps Greece's most famous showpiece, with all its ancient citadels, palladiums, theatres, temples ... and then that other Pompeii-like centre, Delos, one time capital of the Cyclades, legendary birth place of Apollo, worshipped by the ancients as God of Light and Music, and his twin sister, Artemis, Goddess of Hunting ... and of course we must spare time, a week in fact, for visits to Athens, that cultural cradle of the universe, so that we could stand on top of the Acropolis, wander through the famous Plakka district, and spend bemused hours in the National Museum of Athens, with all its priceless treasures. Indeed, it was going to be a summer to remember.

Meantime we had our more immediate life at the Mill House. Suddenly out of the blue, we had a visit from Jess's sister Frances, next youngest of a family of five girls long ago scattered far and wide. One of Jess's sisters, Brenda, had died many years previously, and another, Beryl, had been living in Australia for about twenty years; but the other two, Marjorie and Frances lived up in the Midlands. Once or twice over the years we had seen something of Marjorie, a Medical Officer of Health at Wolverhampton, who had always had a soft spot for Cornwall and periodically paid visits. Frances, on the other hand, though at one time she had lived in Penzance with Jess's mother and knew the county well, had very much gone her own way in recent years. She was now, we had heard, Superintendant of School Meals for the whole of Liverpool, obviously a very important post.

So now when over the long distance telephone Frances told Jess that she and her second husband, Holly, had a few days off and thought of a trip down our way Jess was only too pleased to fix for them to come and stay with us ... albeit slightly apprehensive of how the reunion of the 'kid sister' act would work all these decades later. We need not have worried: Frances and Holly turned out to be cheerful and friendly, very thoughtful guests, and we had a splendid week together, commemorated in the family album, as such occasions usually are, with lovely snaps of groups gathered at such local beauty spots as the Logan Rock, Land's End, Newlyn Harbour, St. Ives, Zennor, etc.

Although we had a spare bedroom where they could have slept we thought it might not be a bad idea to put up Frances and Holly in what had been Stephen's Pad, the tumbledown remains of what had been a large bungalow in the grounds here. Several rooms of the bungalow had been preserved, but in Stephen's day rather forlornly; that winter we had made a big effort to tidy up the area, repairing the plumbing and electric wiring and completely redecorating the kitchen and lounge and bedroom. It was Jess's idea that if we did this we might try letting out the chalet during the summer months thus bringing in a little much needed income.

We had done all the work, and the place was looking remarkably spick and span, especially as I had just completed a rather weary painting of the outside. Much of the earlier work had actually been done by Stephen, and indeed the general idea had been that he would continue to live in the chalet – however two recent developments' had resulted in Stephen being wafted away out of our lives. The first was meeting an American girl Gina, to whom he had become rather visibly attached ... the second, arising out of the first in a way (for Gina was a ballet student in Paris), was Stephen's discovery that he could earn very good money busking with his guitar in the streets of Paris. Consequently after spending Christmas with us, he and Gina had gone off to Gay Paree, from where occasional letters painted on enthusiastic picture of Bohemian life in a big cheap attic room at the top of Hotel Stella, somewhere on the Left Bank, with occasional forays to woo the cinema queues of Champs Elysées and other centres – not apparently, without success, since sometimes Stephen could earn £10 a night. For this he needed a bottler, someone to go round rattling a money box, and here of course, Gina was invaluable, being both pretty and determined. We couldn't help being reminded of a period five years previously when Demelza had done much the same thing in the West End of London – a strange twist to the Val Baker family history.

Anyway, with Stephen away the chalet remained untenanted, and so we offered it, a little tentatively, to Frances and Holly. It was not, we said nervously, exactly luxury accommodation, and we would quite understand if they preferred a more comfortable room in the house. Not at all, they said cheerfully, they didn't mind at all. Funnily enough they didn't either, and seemed to look on the whole experience of staying at the chalet as something very enjoyable – just like a second honeymoon!

With the excuse of Frances and Holly staying with us we were able to make one of our periodical forays into local social life. Fortunately we had been invited to the opening of a show of Margo Maeckleberghe's paintings at the Orion Gallery, Penzance, always one of my favourite spots, so we took Frances and Holly along with us to see a very striking array of paintings by my favourite painter. How I would have loved to own one of those huge Atlantis paintings, mystical outlines of land and women's form all intermingled ... Ah well, at least I had a beautiful smaller one of Margo's, looking across Mounts Bay to the Lizard, which I can see every day in our kitchen.

We were pleased to see at the opening an old friend Jack Pender, another local painter, one of the few – like Margo — to be actually of Cornish birth. Jack belonged to a very ancient Mousehole family and had lived most of his life in that tiny enclosed little fishing port-cum-holiday resort. He really was part of the local community, on first names terms with all the fishermen. His father had been a fisherman before him, and his grandfather – but his grandfather had been something more than just a fisherman, he had painted too, a whole series of striking primitive paintings – a remarkable man in fact, of whom Jack had once written me a fine article in the *Cornish Review*, 'Grandpa was a Painter'

Not long before I had written an article about Cornish painters which had appeared in the *Illustrated London News*, with reproductions of several paintings, including one of Jack's. Partly as a result of this publicity his work had been taken up by the BBC who had decided to feature him in their series, 'One Pair of Eyes', and this very programme was due to be televised in a week or so, so of course, Jack had much to tell us about this. He obviously had appreciated the publicity of the article, and now repeated something he had often said to Jess, a great admirer of his work: 'Look, I promised to give you a painting of mine – when are you going to come and collect?'

'Well, Jack, you know I'd love to, any time.'

'How about this week end, then?'

'I'd love to Jack but – we've got my sister and her husband staying with us.'

'That's all right – bring them alone too.'

And that was how one Saturday morning the four of us came to be wandering through the tiny winding streets of Mousehole, looking for Jack's studio, which we found with considerable difficulty, tucked up a seemingly deserted alleyway. Once inside we were fascinated to see evidences of Jack's recent hard work. Frances and Holly, who had never seen Jack's work before, were even more fascinated – and the upshot of our visit was not only did Jess get her picture, but Frances bought one to take back to Liverpool.

Another night, before they returned, Frances and Holly came with us to have a meal in a new Indian Restaurant which had just opened, of all places, right opposite Newlyn fish quay. From the restaurant's wide windows we could look right out upon the wide doors of the market, now all shut up of course. Both Jess and I spared more than a passing thought for 'the good old days', in the very youth of our marriage, when we owned a ramshackle old house in Morrab Place, Penzance, with rooms let to several of our friends like Len Missen and Anthony Richards, and how every Saturday night the whole lot of us would drive over in old cars to the Ship at Mousehole, stopping on the return journey for some fish and chips at the Gem Cafe – and as like as not, going on to the Saturday night 'hop' at the Fish Market. For, incredible as it may seem now, in those days on many Saturdays in the summer the whole fish Market would be completely cleaned out, sawdust spread on the glistening concrete floors – and, to the tune of a five-piece band, open air dances would take place. They really were gay and marvellous affairs. Entry was only a shilling – so large crowds would come, and there was usually quite a carnival atmosphere. How could there not be, with such a marvellous setting, with all the glittering lights of Newlyn Harbour scattered around and reflected in the dark waters which ebbed and flowed around the very roots of the fish market?

Ah, happy days! Although we have never actually lived there, Newlyn has always occupied a central place in our family folklore. It has always seemed to me the natural successor to St. Ives, the latter now spoiled almost beyond redemption by its inhabitants' mania for tourism – Ye Quick Money Cafes, Ye Olde Gifte Shoppes, Ye Endless Bed and Breakfast. Newlyn is very much a *working* port (which of course is what St. Ives once was) – to this day it remains the second largest fishing port in the West Country, after Brixham, and personally I never tired of taking a stroll along the long long quay, especially if there is rough weather and all the trawlers are in, moored literally in droves.

Many of these trawlers are similar to our own boat which lends a professional interest to my inspection – though, of course, the majority are even bigger, up to 90 and 100ft mark. There is something magnificently satisfying about the aroma of a fishing port, and by that I don't just mean the fish, but rather the smell of ropes and tar and all the other requirements of working boats. The fishermen themselves, too, are fascinating; as they sit mending their nets their brown and wizened faces somehow suggest a lifetime of awesome awareness of the big seas around the Cornish coasts. In fact of course, many of them earn more money these days than many a business executive – but well, as with the miners, good luck to them, theirs is a dangerous job.

Ironically, our personal relationships with Cornish fishermen have never been of the happiest. In my innocence, when we acquired *Sanu* I thought that boat ownership would ensure the friendship of fellow boat owners – this may be so in some parts of the world, but was certainly not so at St. Ives, where we found most of the local fishermen antagonistic. It is all part of a curious Cornish trait of pettiness and jealousy, downright cussedness, which ruins so much of local life. Mind you, St. Ives must be an outstanding example of the darker side of this coin ... where else in the world, in these modern days, would innocent holiday visitors be literally attacked and stoned, or have vicious Alsatian dogs set upon them? This has happened at St. Ives on more than one occasion to large numbers of young men and women whose sole crime is that they wear their hair long and dress in jeans and other 'hippy' clothes.

The hypocrisy of such behaviour is shatteringly summed up by two anecdotes which are verifiable. The first occurred some years ago when an unknown 'hippy', the now famous pop star Donovan, came to St. Ives and was treated in a very unfriendly

fashion by local people. Years later, when famous, he
returned and was given all the honours, staying at the best
hotel etc., Secondly, more recently I couldn't help being wryly
amused to read a remark by a Western Television personality,
David Rodgers, who had been invited to open one of the top
social events of the Year, the St. Ives Trade Fair. 'I wasn't
given quite such a warm welcome on my last visit here,' he
mentioned mildly, going on to explain that *then* he too had the
long hair of a hippy! It is surely a sad comment on the Cornish
that, living in such a beautiful and haunting land, they can
continue to introduce such blemishes of human behaviour.

When Frances and Holly had departed, taking back with
them to Liverpool a rekindled obsession with Cornwall, Jess
and I got down to one of the last jobs in our chalet
improvements. As so often in the affairs of the Mill House, this
had to do with water. The chalet being a good thirty feet
higher than the highest point of our stream we had to find a
way of raising water to fill the huge galvanised tank that stood
in the hillside above the building. We did have a well in the
top field, but the cost of installing an electric pump and piping
would have been considerable, running into hundreds of
pounds. Fortunately we were offered an alternative. Rooting
around in our old workshop Stephen had found the remains of
a strange old water pump ... when he finally cleaned this up
and took it to pieces and put it together again he found, to his
growing excitement, that it was one of those ancient single-
part water pumps which operates almost like a perpetual
motion. Its working principle is rather similar to that on
which a miner's cage-life operates: a pipe runs from the
stream downwards until it enters the main body of our pump,
this latter consists of a circular container, about six inches in
diameter – when this is filled with water a one way valve
closes, holding the water in. The next rush of water from the
outside pipe forces the first lot of water past a second non-
return valve and into a pipe which climbs up and up ... and up
... and up.
Theoretically, for all I know, there might well be no limit to

how high the water can be raised in this fashion – suffice to say it soon rose right up to the top of our distant tank – and so we had our water supply. There were one or two teething problems, necessitating our sending for someone we knew to be an expert with old machinery – Dick Barnes from Lamorna – but after taking a close look at the pump he explained it was really only a question of one or two new washers. Soon the pump was working beautifully, clicking away day and night until it had lifted up about five hundred gallons.

Jess was delighted with the success of the new machine; for my part I could not help striking a note of caution. It *was* a marvellous idea, certainly an economical affair – but supposing it went wrong? Supposing for a variety of reasons it broke down or did not work efficiently – for instance at the height of a dry summer, when perhaps the water might not have sufficient pressure? Or what if the pipe got blocked? Alas, all my forebodings proved well founded, and when later that year we did let the chalet for a few weeks to holiday makers our friend Ben, who was looking after things, had to spend many hours servicing the somewhat temperamental pump. Fortunately it only broke down once for any period of time.

Now with the pipe out of the way, or so we thought, Jess and I embarked on preparations for our own departure. As ever Jess felt a little sad, even a little peeved, to realise that once again she would have to be away from the Mill House just when so many of our vegetables and fruit were just coming to the point of picking. So much the better for Ben, who was caretaking for us while we were away – he would have a rich choice of beans, onions, carrots, lettuce, spinach, potatoes, the lot. Still he would need them to keep up his strength for coping with all kinds of possible problems, like, for instance, Esmeralda and Lulu taking to the local lanes.

Or so we were thinking – when one day Jess caught sight of a strangely appropriate advertisement in the *Cornishman*. '*Wanted*', it read, '*Donkeys for summer work on local beach.*' We could hardly believe our eyes, it seemed too good to be true. Jess at once rang up the telephone number given, and soon a couple of attractive young ladies appeared to explain to us that they hoped to run donkey rides for children and holiday makers on Marazion Beach that summer. They already had one or two horses but felt donkeys were more suitable. They were delighted with Esmeralda and Lulu, and it was quickly arranged that they should have the donkeys for July and August at a nominal sum plus their keep.

'It's an ideal arrangement,' said Jess, with relief. 'It saves Ben all that worry – it means they'll be well fed – and they'll do a bit of walking, do them good.'

Soon the day came when the girls came round with a big horse van and a somewhat apprehensive Esmeralda and Lulu were whisked off to their temporary new life – and we were made even more emphatically aware that our own impending departure was drawing nearer and nearer.

By now the Mill House population was reduced to just Jess and myself and Genevieve, at that time finishing her first year at Redruth Art School. It was near the end of Genny's term and to mark the occasion she was spending hours and hours on a 'project' for the end of the term exam – or to be frank inveigling many of her friends and acquaintances into assisting so that for a couple of weeks the gardens of the Mill House were alive with sounds of youthful laughter, as little Jackie and Francis and Jane and a few other students grabbed brushes and lengths of fibre glass and struts and heaven knows what and helped to create Genny's masterpeice. This was, believe it or not, a labyrinth-like maze structure with an artificial hen at the top from which a ping pong egg ran down and rolled through miles of piping before dropping neatly into a basket at the bottom. I can't remember what the point of it was, but fortunately Genny showed other more lasting attributes, both at painting and sketching and of course ceramic design.

Secretly Jess and I hoped she would continue with her course at the School but alas there were signs of deviation. An old boy friend Sheldon, an American film director, had re-appeared on the scene, with a tempting proposition that Genny should go with him to India to work on some

documentary films out there. At first it seemed very much one
of those up-in-the-air affairs, but when one day Sheldon made
it clear that he was willing to pay for Genevieve's whole trip
and that she could also earn money working on the film, she
began to consider the idea more seriously.

I must say we had to sympathise with her obviously
growing inclinations to 'take off' ... after all at twenty what
could be more exciting or mind-opening than a trip to India,
the Himalayas, Nepal (with prospects of going on to South
America later)?. Even her own teacher at the School of Art
privately told her: 'My God, if I were you I'd jump at the
chance.' And anyway, Genny's work had pleased the school so
much that it was pretty clear she could take a year off and still
come back and resume. Not surprisingly in the end Genny
decided she could do her Indian trip – but only after our
Greek cruise, of course.

Soon the time left for us in Cornwall, that hot and hopeful
June (afterwards it was to rain continuously in Cornwall, as in
most parts of Britain, for practically the whole of June and
August) dwindled to a couple of weeks. Originally there had
seemed plenty of time; now suddenly it was all a neurotic rush
around. One of my worst problems was that I had discovered
that anti-fouling paint in Malta cost something like £12 a
gallon – since we needed five gallons to paint *Sanu*'s bottom,
this represented an absurd extravagance, as I could buy a five-
gallon drum in Redruth from the surplus stores for £12. Our
economics were so tight that I could not afford to miss such a
bargain – but how to carry five gallons of anti-fouling on an
aeroplane?

It sounds improbable, but in fact I achieved just such a
dubious record, by stirring up the five gallon drum and
decanting the anti fouling into five smaller gallon plastic
containers and subsequently burying these in three of our
suitcases. My secret fear was that one of the containers might
leak red anti fouling paint – at that time of hi-jack scares the
sight of 'blood' pouring from a passenger's belongings would
not have made a good impression. In the event, almost

unbelievably the anti-fouling travelled from Heathrow to Malta without either damage or cost – but my arms ached for weeks after.

When the last few days arrived and Genevieve realised that for her the journey was rather more momentous than merely departing for a holiday – she began to have nostalgic second thoughts. Things were not improved by a natural tendency of all her friends to come rallying round to say their farewells. In retrospect I am a little surprised that Genny got away at all.

Even our very last journey to Penzance Railway Station became a curiously touching one. Genny's friend, Ben, drove us from the Mill House with all our baggage, as we had parked away our own car 'for the duration'. When we got to the familiar domed station we found quite an official delegation waiting to see us on our way. There was little Jackie Durrant, with whom Genny had become specially friendly (and who had hopes one day of Genny joining her pottery at Pendeen) – and other girl friends, dark eyed little Jane and vivacious Bernie and folk singer Chris, and Frances and George.

There was even a nice surprise for Jess and I in the familiar presence of our old friend Jack Richards, who had come with us on the boat the previous year, and knew how excited we would be to be off again. Charmingly, all the young people had brought little presents for Genny and sometimes ourselves, just tiny things but so thoughtful that I could see tears were not far from Genny's eyes … as for Jess and I, when we left we were clutching a large bottle of Asti-spumante which Jack thrust into our hands with a wish for *Bon Voyage*.

At last we and our collection of umpteen bags ('What *have* you got in that bag, Denys?' said Jack, mopping his brow after carrying one suit case of anti fouling a few yards along the platform) were safely on the London train. We all came and leaned out of the window to wave a last goodbye to our little circle of friends.

'Goodbye, Genny,' they called. 'Good luck – give India our love.'

'Goodbye,' we all waved. 'Goodbye.'

Suddenly there was a whistle, and the train began to move. For us it was a nostalgic moment; for Genny, who was at the start of a journey of thousands of miles, it must have seemed a good deal more momentous. She remained leaning out of the carriage window long after we had sat down again, waving and waving until at last the bend of the track cut off her farewells forever. When she came and sat down again she looked very sad.

'Never mind,' I said trying to cheer her up. 'Look on the bright side – we're off on a marvellous new adventure.'

And of course before too long we were enjoying lunch on the train and a bottle of wine, and then at Heathrow Gill and Jane had rushed out from London to see us off, Sheldon too, breaking off from a film he was editing – and one way and another time passed in a whirl of excitement until at long last we found ourselves sitting on a big VC 10, taking off into the startling sky for Malta, and dear old, fat old *Sanu*.

VI
Interlude at Malta

At mid-day Jess and Genny and I had been saying our farewells on Penzance station to a group of friends: at midnight on the same day we were landing at Malta Airport, some 2000 miles away! Such is the time-saving wonder of the modern aeroplane (almost the only wonder to my mind). The same journey by a juxtaposition of car, rail and ferry steamer would have taken nearly half a week, if not longer. In previous years we had left *Sanu* at a French port, Agde, up the River Herault, and this had involved at least a two day drive out in our own car, laden to the roof tops with useful equipment for the boat. Now we could only take with us our suitcases (plus that leaden weight anti-fouling!) but at least we didn't waste any time getting to our destination.

Malta, as ever, was hot; even at midnight quite hot. We hailed a taxi and set off to look for *Sanu*. The phrase is deliberately chosen for after coming all that distance it suddenly became evident that I had forgotten *Sanu*'s address. Ludicrous as it sounds, the fact is I knew very well *where Sanu* was, that is I felt sure that *when I saw it* I would recognise the creek where she was berthed, but the exact name of the creek now completely escaped my memory. This is very unusual, as I have an excellent memory, and it is quite possible that this was some last little negative flicker caused by a secret dread of facing up to taking *Sanu* to sea again. Be that as it may Jess and Genny, both by now very tired and simply wanting to get to bed, grew more and more irritable, as, with increasing desperation, I directed the bewildered taxi driver here there and everywhere.

'There ... and I think that may be the road ... On, no it's a cul de sac ... well ... Look, our boat is up a creek, you know with a lot of other boats ...'

My voice tailed away. I was only too well aware that Malta was like one vast marina, with creek after creek stuffed full of elegant yachts in placid rows. Which was the one housing our own beloved *Sanu*? I racked my brain, I had an idea it began with M... but M what?

In the end, as the whole thing started to become ridiculous and the taxi meter clicked higher and higher, I asked the driver to take us right into the heart of Valetta, the big round piazza where all the squat little Malta single-decker buses started. Yes, this was better, now I could get my bearings. We should take *that* road, and then follow *to the left*, and then – ah, yes, there was a sign of a place well beyond where the boat was, Sliema. That would be right, if we took the Sliema road we would eventually come to – what the hell was the name of it?

Further conjecture, fortunately became unnecessary. The taxi swung round a bend and there was the familiar creek – and there, dimly visible by the quayside lights, was *Sanu* herself, on the other side of the water.

The taxi driver, seeing my look of relief, grinned and uttered the magic name of the creek.

'Msida – you wanted. Msida?'

'That's it.' I looked in triumph at my exasperated companions. 'We're here!'

We pulled up beside *Sanu* with a screech of brakes. I saw that there was still a light in the aft cabin. A few moments later we were greated by a relieved advance party of Stephen and Gina, and Llewellyn, younger son of Frank and Kate Baker. They had all been on *Sanu* for several weeks getting on with some much needed repairs and improvements. Llewellyn also had with him his little seven year old daughter Nell, by now fast asleep of course. The two boys came and quickly lugged in our luggage. ('Dad, what on earth? –' said Stephen, lifting up the first of the anti-fouling bags – and grinned when I explained). It was too late to do more than greet one another enthusiastically – and excitedly, thinking of all that was to come – and then Genny went off to find a bunk and Jess and I climbed wearily into our familiar bed in our deck cabin, where Stephen and Gina had thoughtfully laid some sheets and a blanket. Within minutes we were asleep.

The next morning we were up early with the brilliant sun. As always before we could go anywhere we had to give *Sanu* a thorough going over. The previous autumn, during the trip, Jess and I had gone round the boat with Llew, who had been with us then, too, and outlined exactly what we wanted him to do. We were fed up with our perpetual deck leaks; true it never rained much in the summer, but every winter water positively spurted over the interior. We had arranged for Llew to take on the mammoth task of completely stripping down the deck surface (this involved taking up large areas of tough leaking fibre glass) and then sealing the joins between the planks with hot pitch. It had sounded simple enough then but inevitably things had not worked out quite like that. As soon as he had begun taking up the fibre-glass Llew had found several small but worrying patches of wood rot – nothing vast, but specific enough to need completely cutting away and replenishing before proceeding with the pitching. Unfortunately one of these areas had proved to be around the big anchor winch, necessitating the complete removal of the winch, laying of fresh timber and replacement – quite a formidable task, on which Stephen and Llew had worked like Trojans.

All these repairs had taken Llew some time, and now (when I had actually hoped to arrive and find the work done) he was only just able to begin applying the pitch, a Herculean task which was in fact to occupy his unrelenting attention not only for the rest of the time at Malta, but spasmodically during the actual trip.

Leaving Llew to the deck work I joined Stephen in taking a look at the bowels of the boat, that is the engine room. Usually we leave the engine strictly alone for each winter, a course not generally recommended but one which seemed to have served well enough in the past. This time the firm who had very efficiently kept an eye on *Sanu* for us, Yacht Services of Malta, had insisted that it was their practice to run engines once a week, and I had not liked to argue about it, especially as their workmen were very willing, and indeed quite intrigued by our old Kelvin. As a result they had run the engine regularly, no doubt at the cost of considerable physical strain, for starting the hand-turning diesel is a case of art rather than brute strength.

Unfortunately after a while they had found themselves unable to start the engine at all, so that there must be a fault somewhere. Fortunately it was nothing very serious, just the timing out of line, and in the end we got the old brute going again. It always amuses me what affection these old Kelvins inspire – long after she was humming away the Maltese engineer who had been called in stood rubbing his hands together and positively purring with pride and delight.

After Stephen and I had serviced the main engine and the generator we found ourselves urgently needed on other jobs. My particular task for the next ten days was an arduous one. For the first time in our ten years of owning *Sanu* she had been affected by the Mediterranean sun – Malta being, of course, the hottest place we had ever used as a winter berth. What had happened was that the constant beating of the hot sun on the side planks had caused them to shrink so that now it was possible to stand down in the saloon, or in the fore cabin, and see daylight between every plank! They were all above water (otherwise the problem would not have arisen, as the water protected the lower planks from the sun) and there was no danger in port – but once we got to sea and the boat was heaving up and down, water might easily start pouring in.

My job was to mix up enormous quantities of a rather lethal mixture of red lead and putty, take a long roll of cotton string, get into the dinghy, and then move down the side of the boat, first hammering in the string and then spreading over it layers of putty until each long crack was safely filled up – or caulked, to use the nautical term.

Not surprisingly I found the job extremely tedious: understandably as each 'crack' was in fact about sixty feet long. No sooner had I completed one row then I had to go back and start on the next – there were about a dozen on each side of the boat, so that meant several solid days' work. And then at the end of it all I still had to start all over again and paint the sides, this time covering up our previous year's dark navy blue (which we suspected had increased the rapidity of the cracking) with a gay azure blue, which made a pleasant summery contrast with the gloss white of the higher parts of the boat.

Those were pleasant early July days at Malta. The heat was tremendous, usually around 80-85 degrees, sometimes up to 90, and we all worked in shorts and bikinis, and in little Nell's case, nature's beauty. Although it had always been a strict rule of mine that we just could not take very small children on the boat, I had usually specified until the age of seven, so Nell just qualified. She was a sweet little girl who had so far led an eccentric life. Her mother lived in India and Llew in England, so she had spent some time in each country, and several times made the enormous overland journey – indeed this last time, being very broke, Llew had perforce had to hitch-hike with Nell as his companion. Apparently the journey had been much more successful than when he had done it before as a lone male!

One result of this cosmopolitan existence was that Nell was in some ways very old for her age, and this meant that she was sharp and quick witted about everyday life on the boat, and could be very helpful. She could also, alas, be a real chatterbox, and there were times, when we all longed for a brief early afternoon siesta, when any of us would cheerfully have throttled 'talking Nell'. However, let's be fair, on other occasions we were glad enough to send her off on interminable foot slogs down to the nearest cafe to bring back ice-cold bottles of lemonade and Coke, or maybe some of those marvellous Italian-style graffito ice-creams.

We lived quite a routine life on board *Sanu* in those working days of the first two weeks. First to arise, always, was Llew, partly perhaps because, being a fresh-air fanatic, he always slept curled up on a mattress on the wheelhouse roof. Imagine trying to sleep out on a roof in England, you'd be soaking wet within a couple of nights – in Malta they had not had any rain for three months! Not only was Llew a fresh-air fiend, he was also very interested in Zen-Buddhism and other Eastern movements – an interst which led to one comic encounter. As a Buddhist and Yoga follower it was Llew's practice first thing every morning (usually about six o'clock as the sun rose) to stand up on top of the wheelhouse roof and start doing deep breathing exercises at the same time holding his hands high up in the air.

All unbeknown to him these activities did not go unnoticed by occupants of the block of flats across the way. By an extreme coincidence one of them was a policeman, the self same policeman who was once sent to *Sanu* to register an official complaint about the amount of noise the boys had made with a late night party.

'Excuse me,' the policeman had said with great interest, after the complaint was out of the way, 'But is one of you the person who prays on the roof every morning?'

'Er, yes,' Llew had said with a smile. He had been going to explain that these were in fact simply Yoga exercises, when the policeman continued excitedly.

'Really? That's *most interesting*. Tell me, what do you pray *for*? Do you pray to be rich, to make lots of money? Please tell me the secrets of your religion.'

I don't know how Llew got out of that one, but he went on firmly with his rites – and indeed made a rather magnificent spectacle, for he had a fine physique and used to wear no more than one of those Indian briefest of briefs called a Gallotty (inevitably the subject of further calls by the police, for Malta is a Catholic country and extremely prim in many ways).

The rest of us foreswore such spartan activities, but we all worked extremely hard. Soon the results began to show ... by the time the day drew nearer for us to take *Sanu* round to the Manoel Boat Yard for her to be slipped and have the famous anti-fouling applied, our dear old boat was beginning to look quite handsome. Apart from painting the top-sides, we had cleaned up the two masts and the wheelhouse roof, also put aluminium silver paint on all the metal parts, like the anchor and winch and the davits. Jess and I had also had a go at repairing our endlessly troublesome inflatable, the C-craft and the Campari – neither of which, in all honesty, would I ever recommend to anyone, but I may be unlucky. As fast as we patched up one hole another appeared: however, in the end we had both boats useable – provided you were sure to take with you (a) a hand pump (b) a baler.

Now and then we ventured into Valetta shopping for this or that piece of equipment. This involved an extremely cheap passage on one of the dozens of antiquated little coloured buses which rumble endlessly around Malta – a feature of them all being the rosary and Virgin Mary standing behind a glass case, just above the driver's seat. Not only do the Maltese look like the Italians, they must have a lot of Italian blood in them, and they also share the Catholicism and simple religious beliefs.

We have never stayed there more than a couple of weeks but have always found the Maltese very kind and helpful and also surprisingly fiercely proud of their independence. Fortunately from our point of view, old habits die hard and much of the life was still geared up to English visitors, so that we never had any problems over language, for instance.

Among other advantages, we found Malta quite the cheapest country we had ever visited (this despite an iniquitous local arrangement that on every English pound we had to pay tax of 15 pence!) Spain, Italy, Greece, Yugoslavia – you can keep the lot as far as economics go, Malta is far the cheapest. I have never forgotten, as a supreme example, a meal for four we had in a really pleasant, indeed 'posh' restaurant in the heart of Valetta, *The Britisher*, overlooking the harbour. After apéritifs, a five course meal, three bottles of wine and coffees, we were presented with a bill for £3.45! No wonder so many English boat owners keep their boats at Malta, for not only are berthing charges extremely low (and the boat as safe as it could possibly be) but living expenses are correspondingly down. I only wish our feeding costs for the rest of that year's trip could have remained on the Maltese level.

As it was, before leaving we stocked up as much as possible with large supplies of basic things like coffee, cheese, tinned fruits, sugar, etc. We also, with our customary glee, arranged for a large duty-free delivery of spirits (the prerogative of every yacht master on leaving one country for another), including vodka at 70p a bottle, rum the same, and even good class brandy at little more than £1 (plus an extraordinary local brandy supplied at £2.45 for a *gallon!*)

The day we had to move the boat round to Manoel Boatyard produced one of those *Sanu* dramas without which none of our cruises is complete. As befitting the early stages of a cruise this was in a comparatively minor key. The bow of the boat was held not only by ropes attached to a large master chain running down the centre of the quay, but also by our own anchor which had been laid out when we first came to the berth. Unfortunately over the winter the anchor must have dragged in a little so that now, when we came to wind it in, the chain went taut and we realised the fluke had caught firmly on the master chain, twenty feet under water. All our neat little plans to have the boat round at the slip by nine o'clock were thrown out, and for a time it looked as if we would be stuck all day.

Fortunately 'Boss', the genial general factotum of Yacht Services, is a man of great enterprise. He jumped into his familiar white Mini Moke and roared off – to return an hour later accompanied by a skin-diver already dressed in wet-suit and bringing with him an air cylinder. Within minutes the skin-diver had plunged into the rather murky water, kicked up his heels – and lo and behold had found the anchor and attached a line of rope round its stem. We then had to head *Sanu* forward across the creek: all at once the anchor was freed and we were able to haul in the chain and eventually our familiar old fisherman anchor – plus about a hundred weight of pungent Maltese mud.

Still, we were free and off on our short journey round the

point and up the next bay to the shipyard. Or were we?

'Stephen,' I said worriedly. 'Look at the shore – we're hardly moving!'

It was true enough, we were just crawling along.

'Have you got the throttle full out?'

'Of course.' I pushed the lever up to the furthest point – still we meandered along.

'Oh, Lord,' I said, at once overwhelmed with forebodings. 'I'll bet there's something radically wrong with the engine. Probably need new cylinders or something. It'll cost the earth – we'll never be able to afford it. We'll be stuck here all summer, you see.'

I fear that at moments such as this I do give way to a vivid imagination, hence my nickname on the boat of 'Mr Panic'. Secretly I find this a good way of coping with problems, to make them seem much worse than they really are – then I am able to get the maximum relief out of the moments of discovering things are not so bad.

'Go easy, Dad. It's probably just the bottom covered with barnacles and all that. That can knock several knots off our speed, you know.'

Of course Stephen was perfectly correct. When a few days later – thoroughly anti-fouled – we sailed round from the boatyard to the visitors berth to await our embarkation for 'foreign waters', *Sanu* slid through the water like a graceful greyhound, making almost twice the speed of our initial journey. Yes, it had all been the fault of our dirty bottom.

The sight of that slightly distasteful area greeted us later that first day after Manoel Boatyard had with amazing speed hauled our huge 23 ton boat high out of the water, to stand there dripping and naked in the hot afternoon air. Unfortunately, unlike all the other boatyards we had previously visited Manoel had a strict rule that owners of boats must not on any account attempt to do any work to the exterior of their boats while on the slip. In other words, we had to pay their men to scrape and clean and anti-foul our hull.

Economically it was a nuisance, but apart from that we had

no complaints; the men went to work with a will and seemed to do a very efficient job ... using, of course, our carefully hoarded anti-fouling, which we delivered up to them still in its little one gallon plastic containers. The men made no comment – just shrugged and smiled and poured the anti-fouling into large buckets, picked up their long handled brooms and began pasting the anti-fouling in long layers across our planks.

The next day the job was done and we were bundled back into the water as quickly and efficiently as we had been hauled out ... by six o'clock that evening we were tying up round the corner at the visitors berth reserved by the Malta Yacht Marina authority for yachts about to make a passage abroad. Here we had arranged for the delivery of our tinned foods, duty-free drinks and other supplies, including water and diesel fuel. This last item represented a woeful increase in our expenditure as the oil crisis had just erupted and I found myself paying nearly double the previous price of about 13p a gallon. Still, *Sanu* has no sails and we are entirely dependent on diesel, so there was no choice. At least we would be starting out with our big 210 gallon tanks, one each side of the boat, full to the brim.

For our last evening at Malta, it appeared, the authorities had decided to provide us with an official send-off. All unknown to us it just happened to be one of the official firework nights, held every summer – on this occasion at Sliema, which was where the boat was now moored. Little Nell in particular had a marvellous evening watching entranced a whole series of set displays. I must say we enjoyed it all, too, with the aid of some bottles of some excellent local white wine (did I mention that Maltese wine, like everything else, is fabulously cheap, and that this particular wine was available at 18p a bottle, or about 3/6d in our old money!)

Earlier that evening a young Canadian working on one of the big yachts had come over to us and asked if we could possibly give him a lift as far as Corfu. As we were still without half of our ultimate complement of passengers, we could see no valid reason to refuse, and Rod, who seemed a nice enough young man, quickly fetched his rucksack and moved over. He told us, as we sat having a late night cup of coffee, that he had worked his passage on an American yacht from the West Indies across to the Mediterranean, then to France and Italy, ending up in Malta. Apparently there is considerable scope in this way, as yacht owners are often desperate for new help. Although he had been comparatively inexperienced he had been paid £20 a week, plus all keep. Now he hoped to find a similar short term job at Corfu to take him along to Piraeus, or if he was lucky Istanbul. From there it would be a case of hitching overland to India and his ultimate destination of Katmandou, the capital of Nepal.

'Why do you want to go there?'

Rod smiled. 'I have a friend, Dick and we arranged to meet over a drink on Christmas Day – at Katmandou.'

We laughed; it seemed as good a reason as anything – and typical of the casual and free and easy attitude of the young to life which I personally find most attractive. Would that I had had such a freedom in my own youth!

At six o'clock the next morning we were up busily tidying up the deck and loosening our mooring ropes. When all was ready Stephen and I went down, filled up with petrol, and clicked on the magneto. I gave the handle a quick half turn, the engine burst into life on petrol – after half a minute Stephen nodded and opened the four injectors, at the same moment I pulled over the turnover lever – and our old Kelvin's note deepened as the engine went on to diesel. We were off!

It was a marvellous sensation being sea-borne at last, watching the sandy gold outline of Valetta harbour slowly receding and heading across the sunlit waters ahead. As we had every right to expect on a mid July day at the height of summer, conditions were almost perfect, the sea calm save for a slight swell, the sky almost indigo blue, the sun a hot ball of fire. We slid easily through the water, our engine humming with a very healthy note, our bow rising and falling and setting up a long white wake.

After about a couple of hours I went and sat right in the bow of the boat, my favourite position, holding with one hand to the mast stay and staring endlessly into the disturbed waters around the bow – occasionally looking around me for sight of birds or fishes, maybe the odd dolphin. I love that position, it is when I most appreciate owing a boat of my own, having this marvellous access to a whole layer of experience that might otherwise have been denied me.

But with all its attendant little worries! As I stared dreamily down at the bow, following its rhythmical plung up and down into the water, some odd remote little worry started tickling at the back of my mind. I suppose it was that famous 'sixth sense' that one develops. I became aware that I was receiving some kind of intuitive warning, *something was wrong*. Something to do with the bow of the boat – somehow it seemed to be plunging a little deeper into the water than normal – yes, that was it. I looked again, more carefully; undoubtedly that was it!

Suddenly the penny clicked. Quickly I unwound myself from the bow and went over and lifted up the hatch of the bosun's locker – our name for the small forward compartment of the boat, situated right in the bow, where we store all kinds of equipment, gas cylinders, drums of paint, of oil, ropes, shackles, wire coils, suitcases, the lot.

For a moment my eyes could not see properly, changing from bright sunlight to the dark interior ... then I *could* see, and I gave a startled cry. The bosun's locker was half full of water – to a depth of four or five feet!.

'Stephen! Llew! Come quickly!'

I had been tempted to shout out we were sinking, but of course that would have been an exaggeration. Partly for the reason that the bow of a boat is the most vulnerable (as in a collision with another boat) on *Sanu*, as on most boats, there is a water tight compartment between the bosun's locker and the rest of the boat. Even if the bosun's locker was full of water we would hardly sink – however our bow would be well down in the water and the boat would be considerably less seaworthy than she should be. It was not a healthy prospect.

Unfortunately we have no fixed pump to deal with the bosun's locker, so we had quickly to bring up a hand pump we keep-in reserve fixed on a long length of piping, and started working that. It did work, but rather slowly, and in the end we decided it would be quicker to use three buckets and work in a chain – that way, with Llew in the bowels of the bosun's locker, Rod straddling the hatch to take the bucket from Llew, and Stephen at hand to quickly empty the contents over the side, we soon got the water level down to a more reasonable level.

Llew then took a torch and had a good look round, coming up in the end to report that he could see where the leak was, on one of those cracks I had hopefully sealed off. It was slightly above water level, but with the bow rising and falling, water was coming in. However, as it was a calm day he didn't think we would have much trouble in containing the problem, now that we knew of its existence, until we reached Syracuse. Of course, the very contact with water would have the helpful effect of causing the wood to swell – all the same at Syracuse we must be sure to re-seal the leak.

Relieved, we continued on our way. Fortunately the weather did not suddenly deteriorate, and by six o'clock that evening we were tied up alongside the main quay at Syracuse where, the next morning, Llew soon sealed off the leak.

We wasted no time in Syracuse, a port forever damned for us by our experience, soon after arriving, when a gang of small boys amused themselves for a whole Sunday afternoon throwing sizeable sharp rocks at our inflatable in an obvious attempt to sink it. The next day we sailed across to a bay just beyond Cape Spartivento on the southern toe of Italy, there anchoring for the night in a rather beautiful setting made somewhat more remarkable by the appearance of a procession of torch-bearing boats full not only of fishermen but of bearded Roman Catholic priests . . . We had obviously settled in the centre of some local festival, and for a couple of hours the strange procession rowed round and round us, no doubt incorporating *Sanu*'s rather irreligious personnel into the ritual proceedings.

The next morning it was a case of on with the long haul northwards along the undulating coastline, until at last we made our way into the commercial port of Crotonne. Here we planned to spend up our remaining Italian liras on a good meal out, being lucky enough to find a typical unpretentious Italian restaurant that served us with enormous plates of excellent pasta, followed by lush ice-creams – washed down by some of that marvellous cold Italian white wine which to me is so superior to the French. With difficulty we staggered back to the quay side and flopped down for a deep sleep.

At eight o'clock the next morning after dragging ourselves out of bed we soon responded to the cheerful sunlight and busy harbour scene, and began preparing to set forth again – but this time with a difference. This time we were no longer heading north, but turning east – out over the open sea, leaving Italy and aiming for a new land, Greece – with Corfu our first port of call, about 130 miles away.

We had just thrown off our last retaining rope and were slowly moving away from the quay when the skipper of a yacht nearby leaned over his rail and called out:

'Hey, where are you bound for?'

'Corfu,' we called back rather proudly. 'Should be there by morning.'

He gave a friendly wave and then added, almost as an afterthought.

'Good luck! By the way – I suppose you've heard the news? Greece and Turkey have gone to war. It was on the wireless this morning. The Turks have invaded Cyprus … and the Greeks say they will bomb Istanbul.' He gave a last warning wave. 'I should keep a good lookout if I were you.'

With these warning words, still ringing in our ears we sailed thoughtfully out of the harbour and headed out to sea. With so many complicated arrangements already made to meet Frank and Kate in Corfu, Demelza and Diana in Athens, Gill and Alan in Kea – well it was a little late now to think of changing our plans. All the same – well, it wasn't everyday, even on board *Sanu* that we encountered a real live war: and we couldn't help awaiting our landfall at Corfu with considerable trepidation.

VII

Idling in the Ionian

Our first sight of Greece was the winking beam of Othoni Lighthouse on one of the small islands off the north coast of Corfu. We spied the light on the horizon about three o'clock in the morning, and then homed in on it for a couple of hours until faint daylight began illuminating the sky and throwing into relief the larger mountainous shape of Corfu itself. By the time dawn finally broke we were near enough to be able to change course and head for our first landfall, the twin bays of Alip and Ayios Spiridion on the west coast, better known as one of Corfu's most famous beauty spots, Paleokastritas.

It is always exciting approaching a strange new coast, indeed a new country, and on this occasion we had the added stimulant of not being a hundred per cent sure that we were heading for exactly the right opening, for Paleokastritas was merely one of several clefts in the long mountainous coast, and there were precious few other landmarks. I was fairly confident we had held well to our course, however, and all doubts were put at rest as we spied first the monastery of Ayios Spiridionos, and then the old Venetian fortress of Ayios Angelo standing in ruins on a 1000 foot hill – yes, this was the right anchorage.

And a delightful first anchorage it proved to be, with our anchor chain clearly to be seen snaking down some thirty feet or so through crystal clear water, burying into white white sands. It really was everything the guide-book promised, and for two glorious days we just relaxed and lazed around. Then, mindful of our date to meet Frank and Kate, we prepared for the forty-five mile trip around the north coast off the island to Corfu Town. This proved to be a glorious trip, the waters as still as a lake, and one beautiful cove after another unfolding before our delighted eyes.

No wonder Corfu is nicknamed 'the Magic Isle' (it is also 'the enchanted isle' of Shakespeare's last play *The Tempest* – as well as the idyllic setting of the Homeric love affair between Odysseus and Nausica). Indeed Corfu makes an excellent choice for the beginning of any visit to Greece, for at once the island conveys, quite unmistakably, the feel (and even smell and memory) of other worlds, of a time of gods and goddesses, of wild spirits.

Soon we had navigated the northern coast and were approaching not merely the north east tip of Corfu but also – and here we grew a little apprehensive, having had many warnings – within sight and sound of that mysterious Eastern European land of Albania. This country, we had been told, was an unfriendly somehow sinister sort of place, its gunboats constantly prowling up and down ready to arrest any unfortunate yachtsman foolish enough to stray into their territorial waters. Well, maybe, but we saw no signs of anything untoward, and passed safely and soundly through the narrow channel separating Corfu and Albania.

We did not in fact go straight to Corfu Town but chose another day of escapism by turning into the tiny sheltered bay of Kalami, some seven miles before Corfu. This was the result of a literary whim on my part. I had read two or three books by the brothers Lawrence and Gerald Durrell recalling life at their family home on the edge of the beach in Kalami Bay, and thought it would be interesting to take a look. And there, as soon as we entered the bay, was the house, standing well defined and rather lovely on the edge of the beach – no longer the Durrell family home, but a quiet pension for holiday makers. It was altogether a beautiful spot. We anchored and swam and rowed ashore and had some iced drinks at the house, and then strolled along the pebbled beach. I envied the Durrells' childhood in such a spot.

Then on to Corfu Town – and our first taste of 'the war'. To tell the truth we had not thought much more about it during our voyage from Italy, and there had certainly been little signs of anything out of the way at Paleokastritas. At Corfu, however, the signs were unmistakable – not surprisingly as Corfu is a major entry and embarkation port for tourists coming into and leaving Greece. Now, patently, they were mostly anxious to be leaving! At the passport control there was quite a feeling of panic, long lines of harassed tourists queueing up for the next ferry to Brindisi.

These included large contingents of a group we were to come across with monotonous regularity around Greece – what we called the 'back-packers'. These were young men and women, students mostly, usually Americans, bearing on their back elongated tubular rucksacks containing all the belongings and probably a light-weight tent as well, who were spending their summer holidays wandering around the Greek Islands.

Without wishing to deny them such a privilege we did often wish they could have broken the habit of travelling in such large numbers, so that in the end the sight of them became a little like spying some advancing army! We have never forgotten the depressing experience at the tiny Cycladian island of Ios when, after two hot hours climbing up to the Chora, or main town, high up on the mountain side, a quaint whitewashed place of wandering alleyways, we finally reached the one and only town square – to find every available seat in the three or four cafes occupied by 'back-packers', with their confounded baggage spread everywhere! There was neither room for anyone else or for any normal Greek atmosphere.

In Corfu, fortunately, things had not reached this stage, but the sight of the long queue was rather depressing, and our own apprehensions were naturally revived as to whether we would be able to go on with our trip. These were not really allayed when one morning I heard a hissing sound from the tall railings which separated our quay from the outside world, and going over I was greeted in a surreptitious whisper by a lady from the British Embassy. She wanted to know, rather conspiratorily, whether we had 'had any trouble' with the Greek authorities. When I said we had not she shook her head dubiously and said, 'Well if I were you I'd lie low for a bit, the British aren't very popular, you know, the war, Cyprus and all that'. She gave me her phone number and said we should get in touch if we had any problems. Fortunately I never needed to make such a phone call, but on reflection I was duly impressed that 'our' government had been sufficiently concerned to come and worry about our welfare.

In fact the war did not really bother us, either in Corfu or anywhere else, though we heard stories later of other yachts facing difficulties, particularly those unfortunate enough to have been originally in Turkey. One such yacht, on arriving at Rhodes, was more or less commandeered by the local Greeks and searched from top to bottom. In Crete, too, we heard tales of English speaking yachtsmen (more notably the Americans, who appeared to receive the brunt of the blame for the Greeks' troubles in the war with Turkey) being spat upon and generally having life made difficult for them.

We, as I say, were fortunate enough to escape this sort of thing, and our closest contact with the war took place here in Corfu when for two or three days we watched endless convoys of motor lorries arriving full of young Greek soldiers hastily call up, on their way to board troop ships for Cyprus. They all looked very young and rather bewildered, and at the docks were often greeted by wailing crowds of relatives. These initial departures must have depleted Corfu's manpower quite a lot, for we heard that 1200 young men were taken away in two days.

Our own touches of drama at Corfu concerned different fields of activity. On a more immediately practical level we had considerable troubles with the harbour itself, which we discovered – too late – to be just about the most unsatisfactory and most badly protected harbour in the whole of the Mediterranean. I don't know what idiot designed Corfu's quite large harbour but he certainly deserved hanging drawing and quartering for managing to create a harbour that offered complete and utter shelter from all winds *except* the one prevailing north to north western wind. As this blew for most of the time, usually starting up at mid-day and continuing until well after dark, we learned to dread its first faint intimations – knowing that in due course great gusts of wind would blow down upon us and our fellow yachtsmen, driving us relentlessly against the quay. Often we were occupied for several hours just trying to keep our boat's stern from pounding against the quay, and we grew thoroughly fed up with the condition.

Fortunately there were times when the wind died down; and then, for much of the time, we pursued our fascinating acquaintance with 'Peter the Greek'. We met Peter in the first place out of curiosity, as he happened to be the owner of a boat we spied immediately we came into Corfu harbour – for the very simple reason that it was identical to our own, in fact one of the British Admiralty's first batch of 50 MFV's, built in 1942. Not only was she obviously the same length and breadth (60 foot on the water line by 18 foot beam and $7\frac{1}{2}$ draft) but she was even painted navy blue and white, our own colours the previous year.

Later on the day of our arrival, when we had tied up securely, with Stephen and Llew I sauntered along the quay and stood looking approvingly at this sister ship. We were of course dying for an opportunity to go aboard and have a look round: as if in answer to our thought a tousled dark head poked out of the wheel house and a voice said, 'Looking for me?'

That was how we came to make the acquaintance of Peter, forty years old, ship's captain – and professional smuggler.

Once we had explained that we owned the MFV which had just come into harbour · Peter was friendliness itself, and insisted on our coming aboard on a fascinating tour of inspection. It did not take as long as a similar tour would have taken of our boat, with all its divided-off cabins, for Peter's MFV was structurally very much as it would have been when the Admiralty sold it off after the war – basically one huge hold in the forward part of the boat, a large midways engine room dominated by a formidable old Gardner diesel, and a large aft cabin, the sort often found on fishing boats with bunks for 6-8 fishermen. On deck was a small wheelhouse with a cabin behind which Peter used for living accommodation.

'But' we said rather puzzedly as we sat round having a drink of wine, 'If your boat's unconverted, what do you use it for?'

Peter grinned quite cheerfully and answered without hesitation.

'Smuggling, of course.'

He told us, then, his story. When he was much younger he had been an engineer on one of the big oil cargo ships. One terrible day, while the ship was moored off Bahrain, there was an explosion aboard and Peter, covered with burning oil, was blown into the sea. By the time he was rescued he was in a pretty bad way, was rushed to hospital and remained there, at first on the brink of death, later slowly recovering, for nearly six months. During this time he had innumerable skin grafts, the result of which were plain to see to this day; when he was finally discharged, as was only right, he received a handsome lump sum in compensation.

With that money Peter bought a powerful motor boat and began smuggling on a small scale. He must have been rather green at the game then: before long he was caught by the Italian police and given a three year prison sentence. His boat, of course was confiscated, though at the end of his sentence the police said to him he could have the boat back if he paid £10,000. Peter had had plenty of time to think about his future in prison and he had made up his mind exactly what he needed – and it was something much more formidable than his old boat. So he told the Italian police what they could do with the boat – and went off on the long journey from Corfu to Southampton in England, where he had seen advertised a sale of Admiralty MFV's. One of these he bought pretty cheaply for a couple of thousand pounds – and now he was sitting in its deck cabin.

Why had he chosen an MFV? Well he would tell us. There were in fact several reasons. First, he had often seen them in action and been impressed by their great stability and sea worthiness. Second, although they were large enough to carry a big cargo, as far as smuggling went, they could still be handled by two or three people. And thirdly – Peter gave a knowing smile – being *wooden* boats they did not show up on the Italian patrol boats' radar screen as quickly as a steel boat.

With this newly acquired vessel Peter had built up a smuggling business as regular and smooth-working as – but much more profitable than – almost any normal legal business. Although he used Corfu as a base for keeping the boat he was careful not to offend in any way against local procedures. The Greek officers of the port knew perfectly well what his occupation was but since he was not breaking any Greek laws they simply left him to it.

Peter employed two young Greeks to help him, and with them aboard, twice a month he set off from Corfu and travelled up the Adriatic coast to a small Yugoslavian port. Ostensibly he was on a general sort of trading trip; in reality he had contacts with some Yugoslavians from whom he purchased supplies of American cigarettes at a fixed price of £30 for cartons of 10,000. As Peter confessed that he sold every carton for £75, it was obviously very much a worthwhile operation.

Once loaded up with his cargo Peter then headed back down the Adriatic, but this time west rather than east – in other words, making for a chosen spot off the Italian mainland. This was when he had to be careful in his navigation, for safety depended on the fact that the Italian patrol boats were powerless to interfere with him so long as he kept outside Italian 12-mile territorial limits. Peter used to heave-to a mile or two on the right side of these limits, and then lower a powerful speed boat which was carried on his MFV's foredeck.

Meantime he would have been in touch on the radio telephone with his Italian contacts on the mainland to arrange a rendezvous – at night of course to have the protective cover of darkness. The speedboat would be loaded up with its first section of tobacco cartons, and off it would zoom into the dark. Aboard the speed boat, once he was inside territorial waters, Peter was a potential target for any prowling patrol boat – but at 40 mph the big Johnson outboard could quickly lose any pursuer.

After delivering the first cargo Peter would go back to the MFV and quickly take on a second load. Unloading time might vary, but would probably involve three or four runs, each one taking anything up to an hour to complete, so it was a long night's work – but of course a profitable one. Skirmishes with patrol boats were more likely than not, but Peter had become increasingly adept at avoiding even the initial contact. The more accomplished he became, the more furious the Italian sea-police's reaction. Recently they had even taken to using the services of a helicopter which would come and 'buzz' Peter's stationary MFV.

It was at this stage we learned the reasons for Peter, a Greek, flying the strange and unfamiliar flag at the rear of his boat. It was what might be called a 'flag of convenience', belonging to a tiny republic called Mali, on the African coast. Apparently Peter had just walked into a Mali counsel office, registered his boat and automatically qualified to fly the country's flag. It was just one more of the several means he adopted for confusing his pursuers. Another method was to be constantly painting and repainting his boat, and even to put one name on the front and another at the back. At the moment it was navy blue and white ...

The penny suddenly clicked in our minds and we recollected an incident in our own cruising career which had baffled us ever since it occurred last autumn. We had been travelling from Syracuse to Malta by night and had been startled, and later most annoyed, to be stopped by an Italian patrol boat which circled round us, bathing us in searchlights, and generally treating us as potential criminals. Only after my indignant protests had the patrol boat finally let us go. Now, of course, all was clear. At that time *we* had been painted navy blue and white: and the Italians had clearly mistaken us for Peter!

When we told Peter this little anecdote he was consumed

with laughter and announced that he would in future paint the name *Sanu* on the bow of his boat.

We had many similar chats with Peter during our stay in Corfu and learned more about the curiously ambivalent attitude of the Greek officials to smuggling. Apparently Peter's occupation was not an oddity, but quite common. At the nearby mainland port of Preveza, he assured us, there were no fewer than 40 full-time smugglers, each with a well equipped motor boat, in full operational order – each carrying out very similar missions to his own. In fact he said with a grin, eyeing Stephen and Llew meaningly, if any of us wanted a job he could give an introduction to his friends at Preveza.

We all became very fond of Peter the Greek. Among other things, he was extremely wise and astute politically, and on the right side of the fence. He hated the Greek junta, delighted in their sudden collapse – and told us sad stories of their oppressions, including the shooting down in cold blood of some 200 Athens university students (it had all been hushed up at the time). I suppose he might be called a criminal, but he dealt fairly harmlessly in cigarettes, took many risks, and was such an engaging human being that none of us could really find fault. We were all very sad when the time came to leave, and Peter came to the quayside and threw off our ropes and waved a rather endearing farewell.

Apart from our encounter with Peter – and of course the little matter of a war going on, plus our berthing difficulties! – our stay in Corfu was a pleasant one. Historically Corfu had come strongly under Western European influences, having been ruled first by the Venetians, later the French, even the British. The town itself was rather lovely, the old quarter specially fascinating, with its maze of narrow streets with tall arcaded houses, balconies, fruit barrows, lines of washing etc. Here one could step from an elegant French boulevard into a Neopolitan back street, and then again emerge before some unmistakably English architecture – or perhaps a Greek Orthodox Church. Restaurants abounded, and there were numerous local specialities – maridaki (whitebait fried with lemon), barbounia (red Mullet), bourdette (boiled fish with red pepper sauce) and pastitie (macaroni pie). Souvlaki and moussaka (meat on a spit and minced meat and bechmel sauce) were other dishes we found popular. Unfortunately I, as a vegetarian, fared rather badly in Greece, even an omelette being regarded as a rare speciality – and almost inedible when made owing to the Greek's curious habit of swamping everything in oil.

From Corfu we made the natural progression of the 25 miles voyage southwards to the next Ionian island of Paxos. We had by now collected Frank and Kate Baker, though only after they had endured a nightmare rail trip across Switzerland and Germany and Italy to Brindisi, and then a troublesome voyage across – never mind, here they were, both looking pale and rather worn with their 'English' complexions, by comparison to our brown and sunbathed countenances. Kate worked very hard as a school teacher and invariably arrived on *Sanu* looking quite deathly – yet within a few weeks both she and Frank would perk up marvellously. One of the reasons, of course, was the *Sanu* routine of 'bathing off the side', which we followed whenever we were anchored at some lovely spot, such as Kalami. Frank, in particular, was a great swimming enthusiast, and was usually the first up in the morning. Lying in our cabin Jess and I could hear a tremendous splash and then the marvellous sound of Frank treading water and singing Latin *Te deums* in a deep baritone voice.

At first, Frank used to go into the sea wearing a very ancient and rather distinguished pair of black and gold swimming shorts, but later on in our trip many of us got in the pleasant habit of bathing in the nude. Frank was one of these, but had to pay for his temerity at one port where, even though his swim in the nude took place at 6.30 in the morning it did not escape the eagle eye of a solitary early fisherman – who must have hurried away to report at once. Later that day an official deputation came to the boat on behalf of the local priest to command that no such goings on should be allowed again! Frank, a lapsed but in his own way a faithful Catholic, was very contrite … for a few days anyway.

Jess and I were glad to welcome Frank and Kate back into the *Sanu* fold, if only because their presence helped to redress the age balance. While I have to admit that being constantly surrounded by 'the young' (which from our middle aged pinnacle means anything between 18 and 30) does in a curious way keep us younger in outlook – I also must confess that there come many moments when we long for the company of someone else who, like ourselves, want just to stretch a weary limb, nod a sleeping head, doze away the fitful autumn of life, etc. Frank and Kate had been coming on *Sanu* with us for the past four or five years and we were all comfortably familiar with one another ... Or were we? The odd, sometimes comic, sometimes slightly disturbing thing about life aboard *Sanu* is that things are not always predictable. Caught up into the tiny microcosms of our nautical world we become subject to intense pressures and counter-pressures of the sort only comparable to tightly-knit family life. ('Mummy, Genevieve's got five more peas than I have, it's not fair ... etc'). Such conflicts could affect even our relationship with old friends like Frank and Kate: fortunately over the years we had developed routines both for leading up to various flashpoints and also for safely journeying away from them.

In the case of Kate, almost all confrontations aboard *Sanu* were sparked off by the vexed question of 'the plank'. Although one of the fittest and strongest sixty year olds we have ever met, thinking nothing of a five mile tramp into the hills, Kate unfortunately suffered a little from a slight unsteadiness on her feet, which could cause complications when going off or on the boat. Partly for this reason we had a very long plank which, whenever we were berthed in a port, we ran from the stern to the quayside, the idea being that Kate could get off more easily (as well as the rest of us of course).

Sometimes 'the plank' worked, and all was well; sometimes, alas, because of the height of the quay (or lack of) things were more traumatic. If the plank was on too much of a slope, or seemed to extend over a particularly fearsome stretch of water, Kate would tend to become rather paralysed, and there would be a great crisis as she hovered at the point of no return. We usually managed with one person standing with outstretched hand at one end and another desperately manoeuvring Kate forward from the other. The problem became more acute if 'the plank' could not be used and there was no alternative to Kate descending by ladder into the dinghy.

Then there would be helping hands in every direction, the boat had to be held steady as a rock and there would be audible holding of breath as Kate's uncertain wobbling foot felt down for the final floor of the boat. Getting back from the dinghy on to *Sanu* could be an even more alarming experience, as the sea's swell constantly tugged at the dinghy. We could never quite understand Kate's worries, as she was a very strong swimmer, but anyway she never actually fell into the sea – though poor old Frank did one rather comical occasion when he was holding with one hand to *Sanu*'s ladder, the other to Kate in the dinghy, and a sudden surge of the sea sent the dinghy swinging outwards. Plonk! went Frank into the fortunately warm ocean.

It seems incredible now, looking back in nostalgic sweet memory, but there were times when tempers grew madly heated over the most minute if admittedly 'fraught' experiences. Poor Kate, usually the kindest and most thoughtful of people, would sometimes be provoked beyond endurance by her struggles to get on and off *Sanu*. One memorable day she lost her temper completely and screamed at me: 'I've a good mind to throw your ladder into the sea! What's more, I'll – I'll jolly well sink your dinghy!'

At the time such scenes could be quite devastating and terrible; five minutes later Kate would be back to her sunny self and almost unaware that we had had 'a row'! In Frank's case it was more a case of fluctuations of mood, something from which I also suffer (my own usual practice, which I am sure the rest of the ship's company find very annoying but it can't be helped, it has therapeutic value, is simply to walk away to a quiet corner and sit looking out across the dark waters, or maybe up at the mysterious star-lit sky). Sometimes Frank would alternate between one day of immense vivacity and happiness, keeping our spirits all on the bubble of happiness – and the next day sinking into what is commonly known as a 'slough of despondency'. Usually on such occasions Frank would retreat to his cabin and lie in melancholy state in his bunk, meditating upon the woes of the world and shaking his head sadly when I took him in a soothing cup of tea.

More likely than not Frank's depression would be due to the inevitable two-or-three-times-a-trip-philosophical-argument with Jess – arguments in which sometimes Kate, sometimes Stephen and other members of the crew would join in – but which fundamentally were between Frank and Jess. In reality they were deeply fond of one another – but you would never have thought so on those candle-lit evenings in the saloon, as with eyes flashing and fist pounding on the table Jess would shriek, 'Religion is the opium of the masses, as *you very well know*. I despise you and your God!' to which with rather ham-acted dignity Frank would draw himself up, hold his aristocratic nose high in the air and remark, 'There is *no* point in continuing this discussion any further. I shall be leaving the boat at the next port.' And so on and so on ... Many of those often hilarious contretemps are recorded for posterity on tapes (and also some none of us would want replayed!)

After recording all these perhaps slightly waspish memories my mind suddenly switched to some long night voyage, when we were all tired and a little dispirited by rough weather, and suddenly miraculously Frank appeared up the wheelhouse stairs bearing hot cups of tea ... or, undeterred by all the vagaries of the weather, good old Kate looked blithely out of the window and said confidently, 'I do believe it's all quietening down. We'll soon see land and be out of all this' – or Frank, again, with an eagle eye for such things, spotting some errant distant lighthouse or the shape of land for which I have been desperately searching without avail. Remembering such times, and our other memorable shared experiences, I realise how much part of the *Sanu* mythology Frank and Kate have become!

So we come to Paxos: five miles long and perhaps a couple

of miles across, the smallest of the main Ionian Isles, but none
the worse for that. In many ways we were inclined to think it
the most perfect of all our berths. Certainly it had the most
remarkable approach from sea. For a long time we could not
believe we would ever find Port Gayo the main town and port
– until at last we spied a very narrow crack in the cliffs and,
following what seemed rather like a shallow river round a
couple of bends (passing through dangerously shallow water
of a depth of 10 feet or so), we suddenly swung round into the
most delightful and picturesque little harbour, the main quay
being also the village square!

Beforehand I had rather assumed Port Gayo would be fairly
deserted ... to my dismay there was quite a small forest of
yacht masts lining the quay. Too late, I realised that stern-to
berthing was going to present more than its usual problems.
With some difficulty we managed to manoeuvre *Sanu* round
into a position roughly opposite the only remaining space, at
that moment dropping our anchor – meantime Llew had got
into our dinghy, along with five lengths of rope tied into one
stretch, and was rowing like mad for the quay in order to tie
the rope up for us to start pulling in our stern. All went well
until Llew landed and then discovered there was just nowhere
to tie the rope until it had been pulled further on to the quay.
Fortunately we saw some of the men from a nearby boat come
swarming along to give a hand: soon there were six hefty men
handling the rope, pulling and pulling ... and pulling ...
Suddenly there was a mighty twang on the rope – the free end
came curling back towards *Sanu* – and on the quayside six
hefty bodies went rolling backwards! One of the rope joins
had given way ...

All this, as usually happens, had attracted the inevitable
amused pack of spectators, who now stood around expectantly
waiting for Act Two. Rather ostentatiously Stephen climbed
up onto the side of the bulwark, poised with hands in the air
and dived into the water. Quickly he swam over to collect the
two ends of rope and join them up again ... than handing the
other end back to the boys on the bank. With much heaving
and pulling *Sanu* was tugged into her berth.

Stephen waved cheerily to the grinning spectators.

'Next time we'll do it all in fancy dress!' he called out, not without an edge of bitterness. We have all come to dread this business of stern-to berthing, as *Sanu* simply will not respond reliably in reverse gear.

Once we were tied up we looked around to thank our helpers from the adjoining boat – and could hardly believe our eyes. Here was yet another MFV of *Sanu*'s class and year! It seemed quite incredible that at two successive Greek ports we should encounter two MFV's. We wondered momentarily if the whole of Greece was given over to our favourite boat – in fact never again on the trip did we come across another ordinary MFV, though here and there we encountered boats modelled on MFV lines.

This particular MFV interested us a good deal more than Peter's boat because it had been converted very practically for Mediterranean life. The owners were a group of cheerful Americans, some of whom had teaching jobs in Athens. They had bought the boat pretty cheaply in Piraeus and spent a whole winter converting the interior. We were full of envy as we stepped immediately, while still on deck, into a large and spacious saloon, comfortably fitted with seats and couches, and with a modern galley adjoining – both leading conveniently up into the neat wheelhouse.

Such an arrangement was eminently suited to life in a hot country, it meant that everyone spent the whole day on deck level, viewing the surrounding sights, eating together, all at deck level. What a pity we had not some such layout on *Sanu*, we thought. Instead our boat was geared up to North European living, with our large and indeed very comfortable saloon below deck, tucked away, rather dark – not the sort of place anyone wished to occupy, on hot Mediterranean summer days, (indeed we spent all our time on deck, and had our meals on the stern of the boat under a large orange awning).

After we had spent an hour going round the Americans' MFV we were all determined to reconstruct *Sanu*'s entire layout. We then took the Americans back to inspect *Sanu*: to our amazement, within a short time they were completely sold on *our* layout and quite seriously talking about scrapping all their plans and doing their boat on *Sanu*'s lines! The grass is always greener ... I could see their point better after we inspected the minor hell-holes of their tiny below-deck bedrooms, in which sleeping on hot nights must have been murder – whereas on *Sanu* we had fewer and larger cabins, some on deck, which make life easier. On the other hand we all felt quite certain that having a big saloon on the deck is much the best arrangement for a hot country.

Ironically, whereas we had come from Malta and were heading for Piraeus – the Americans had left Piraeus and were heading for Malta. Our fortuitous encounter, which enlivened our stay in Paxos, needless to say, was a case of 'ships that pass in the night' – and part of the magic of cruising. Soon we ourselves were off again, this time heading for Levkas, a very different sort of place to Paxos. For one thing it was only an island by virtue of a canal cut through the swampy area which originally connected with the Acarmarian coast. This canal, starting by the Venetian fortress of Santa Maura in the North and ending by Port Drepano in the south, was originally conceived by the early Corinthians, re-dug by the Romans, and finally opened up permanently to shipping in the 18th century.

To travel through its four miles in *Sanu*, with shallows down to ten foot on either side, was quite an experience. All around us the views were striking, for Levkas is very mountainous, with a centre ridge rising to 3,700 feet running from east to south west. The north and west coasts were bare and uninviting but opposite the mainland the valleys opened outwards, the shore and country was green and attractive, studded with orange and olive groves.

Partly because of the worry of all those shallows, partly because of a curious air of seediness and desolation about the main town, none of us felt very happy at Levkas. The wind moaned, we had a very bad berth, almost touching rocky protuberances, even our meal of the night went wrong. We were all relieved to be on our way through the snaking canal

... though I was less relieved, still expecting *Sanu* to ground at any moment.

At last we were out at the other end – and on our way to one of the hopefully high spots of the trip, the fabled island of Ithica, where so legend had it Odysseus reigned in a lofty palace from which he could look out across the sea to his subject islands. But that lay some way ahead: first we threaded our way down the breathtakingly beautiful coastline of Levkas, passing on the south western corner the famous broken white cliff known as 'Sappho's Leap' – a 200 foot perpendicular cliff from which Sappho sang her love songs before leaping for her life. It was a remarkable sight, made more interesting for us by the knowledge, culled from one of our many guide books, that the leap had also been used, during the Festival of Apollo, as a place from which they cast down criminals into the sea ... to break their fall birds were attached to the criminals and if they reached the sea without injury then boats would put out to recover them and they were freed.

On and on, weaving between green and pleasant islands and islets – until about midday we glided gently within a stone's throw of a very famous place indeed, the private island of Skorpios, owned by none other than Mr Aristotle Onassis, the Greek millionaire, a place less startlingly attractive than I had expected, indeed with its rather unnatural acres of closely planted trees seeming rather like a fortress ... still no doubt full of home comforts! We watched through the binoculars and saw the tall masts and graceful shape of the Onassis yacht, *Christina*, and the distant outline of a gracious and elegant house. Then *Sanu* had swept on her way, and we were heading out into more open sea, the sun shining ahead of us like a blazing beacon, beckoning us on and on and on ...

VIII
A Wedding at Sea

'And when arose the brightest of all stars, which heralds the dawn, the sea-wandering bark drew near the Island of Ithica.' So wrote Homer a good many years ago: and, repeating his journey in the late twentieth century, we were equally delighted and astonished by the beauty of this legendary island. Few approaches have had so much to commend them, scenic-wise, as *Sanu*'s leisurely sail between towering mountains into the Gulf of Mola, leading to the island's picturesque capital of Port Vathy.

True, we were a little disconcerted as we approached the anchorage to find much of the available space impressively occupied by one of the most enormous and beautiful sailing schooners we had ever set eyes on – probably three times *Sanu*'s length, a truly gigantic craft, swarming with white uniformed cadets, one of those Swedish Tall Ships on a Mediterranean cruise ... Fortunately – whether by accident or because they did not like to be associated with a rather tatty old English MFV we shall never know – just as we approached so the big schooner began quietly moving out, leaving us free to anchor gloriously in the middle of a sheltered bay.

Here we stayed an enchanted few days, periodically rowing ashore on some expedition – such as one lovely evening's climb high up into the mountains searching for Odysseus's Palace, 'the Grotto of the Nymphs'. The track wound up and up, round and round, and some of us fell by the wayside – Frank and Kate very sensibly settled half way on a stone wall, devouring the fabulous view of mountainous slopes falling down to deep indigo sea. When we finally go to the cave it was very disappointing, notable more for the thousands of initials and messages scratched on the stone walls: not beautiful at all, and retaining very little atmosphere. Still, once upon a time ...

'Once upon a time' makes a good cue line for our next adventure, for it represented a new departure for the captain of the good ship *Sanu*. Earlier in the year Stephen had met and wooed a pretty American girl, Gina, and brought her with him on the trip – now, rather romantically, they wanted me to carry out a wedding ceremony aboard *Sanu*. I had always had the vague idea that ship's captain *could* perform such a ceremony, but now I began to wonder just how much of a ship's captain one had to be before the proceedings to be legal. Buried deep in the heart of fabled Ithica it seemed impossible for me to check up on such a fine point. After some hesitation I decided that since Stephen and Gina seemed very much in love, and could always get married more officially on their return to 'civilization', there didn't seem any harm in going through with what in fact proved to be a touchingly beautiful ceremony.

Naturally everyone aboard *Sanu* was soon geared up for such a special occasion. The first item to be decided was the venue for the wedding. Port Vathy we felt to be a little too normal and official – what we wanted was a completely deserted stretch of coastline, far from the madding crowd. According to the rules of general maritime law, I think we should have been well out at sea, but that would have been practically impossible in an area bound by so many islands: so we chose, as the next best thing, an incredibly beautiful cove known as Pera Pigadhi, off the eastern tip of Ithica.

I often think back to *Sanu*'s slow approach to Pera Pigadhi, at about four o'clock on a shimmering July afternoon. The coastline consisted of a series of rearing mountain cliffs broken here and there by a thin valley – then at last we saw the cove we were aiming for, the water so deep that we had to go quite close in to be able to anchor, even then in depths of forty feet.

The water was absolutely glassy, we could see the bottom quite clearly – ahead of us a white sandy beach, all around tall cliffs covered with heather. It was an idyllic spot, most suitable for an idyllic event.

Such occasions, however, require careful planning. Genny and Llew had volunteered to see to the catering side, and apart from preparing a meal for later on in the evening Genny had whipped up a wedding cake on which Llew had executed a complicated floral design worthy of an ex-student of Falmouth Art School. For liquid refreshments we had bought three large bottles of the Greek equivalent of Asti-Spumante, and they had been cooling off all day. Next there was the question of the bride and groom's attire. We had not exactly come out to Greece with a vast selection of clothes; what we had were mostly summertime shirts and shorts, that sort of thing – so some kind of improvisation was necessary.

In the end Stephen appeared in white jeans and open shirt, with a bright red sash wound round his waist – Gina, more decoratively, was ensconced in an extraordinary combination of some sort of petticoat covered with an enormous length of muslin which Jess had brought on the boat as a mosquito net for spreading over our bed every night – but which now gave just the right wedding-day touch. A piece of this was also torn off and used to attire little Nell, who was the official bridesmaid – her father being the best man. Finally, as the officiating officer in the ceremony, I wore my best summer suit crowned by an enormous Spanish sombrero which happened to have been left on the boat from a previous trip.

By six o'clock all was ready. The sun, which had been almost unbearably hot, had just mercifully sunk behind one of the taller mountains, leaving us with a pleasant cool evening light. *Sanu* wafted gently at her mooring, not a ripple disturbing the sea: everywhere there was hush and beauty, warmth and affection. Up in the bow of the boat I stood in readiness, my sombrero pushed back to give me a better view of the proceedings. It was a long time since I had been to a wedding ceremony – indeed I was inclined to think the last time had been twenty-five years ago when Jess and I were married at South Kensington Registrar's Office – and I had a rather dim memory of the spoken lines, but fortunately Frank and Kate were a little more accurate in their remembrances of such things past. Between us we had had one or two 'run throughs' and managed to produce a fairly reasonable sequence of rhetorical questions. 'Do you Stephen Val Baker take this woman Gina Brown to be your lawful wedded wife … in sickness and in health … etc., etc.?'

Beforehand I had been inclined to be a little jittery about the whole thing, more than once wishing fervently I had never agreed to Stephen's request. In the event, perhaps not altogether surprisingly in the face of all that beauty around, all that affection aboard, the ceremony not only passed off without a technical hitch, but was curiously moving. After I had read out the basic marriage vows and Gina and Stephen had repeated them after me slowly and clearly, Llew had produced not one but two rings, which the bridal couple laughingly exchanged: then Kate – a former Shakespearean actress – stood up and in a lovely resonant voice recited one of Shakespeare's famous love sonnets. As the last cadence of her voice died away on the fragrant early evening air, that was the signal for boisterous congratulations, everyone kissing everyone else, three cheers for the bride and groom. Out came the three carefully guarded bottles of sparkling wine, glasses appeared, and we all drank long and lasting toasts to the happiness of the slightly abashed Stephen and Gina.

Responding to the spirit of the occasion Stephen and Gina then threw off their wedding clothes and dived over the side of the boat into that marvellous warm sea, and swam over to the shore … there to sit, leaning against a rock, staring dreamily into their own private future.

I have failed miserably, I see at once, to capture the strange atmosphere of my one and only marriage at sea … because, I suppose, the things that I seek to capture can hardly be pinned down to paper. Beforehand, as I say, I had some misgivings: what had begun almost too lightly, not as a joke exactly, but in something in the spirit of good humour, might easily have proved a fiasco. To all our reliefs, this was not so.

For Stephen and Gina, obviously, this essentially private ceremony, carried out in such a beautiful setting, among loving friends, did acquire a meaning and significance quite beyond its dubious legal status. At the end of it all, undoubtedly, they *felt* married, which is really all that matters. For us who had shared in the simple proceedings there was a lesson in age old ordinary wisdom: it is not so much the way you do a thing that matters, what matters is *why* you do it. If Stephen and Gina had not been in love, then the ceremony would have been meaningless and unworthy. As it was they cared and we cared – and so they were married.

Certainly no one could have asked for a more beautiful setting for a wedding, official or otherwise. Long after the light had vanished that night we stayed on deck under a magical star-lit sky, marvelling at our good fortune to be here in Ithica, perhaps along with Odysseus and all his Nymphs! It was very late that night before we finally went to bed – after one of the most memorable days not merely of our trip, but of our lives.

After such an event to stay in Ithica would have seemed anticlimatic – anyway it was time to be on our way. Now we were leaving the Ionian Isles, turning east, heading up the Gulf of Patra on a journey which would ultimately take us through the Corinth Canal and into Piraeus itself. But first we had a date – no, not with destiny, but with Delphi. Possibly the most famous archaeological site in Greece, Delphi is not by the sea, but some 30 miles inland among the mountains: we felt we could not possibly pass by without paying a visit, so we decided to call in at one of the nearest ports, berth the boat and take a day trip up to explore the ruins.

Galaxhidi the port we had chosen because it was supposed to offer the best shelter, proved quite the reverse in our experience. From the moment we entered the narrow cul-de-sac creek of a harbour to the time we thankfully left the wind blew hard and we were only able to survive in any comfort owing to the fortunate fact that the ferry boat service had been discontinued and the old ferry quay was available for us to berth alongside. Here we spent some uncomfortable times buffeted about: but at least we achieved our aim of seeing Delphi.

Fulfilling this ambition involved me in doing something I loathe, that is arising at the crack of dawn, literely at 5 a.m., in order to be sure of catching the 6 a.m. bus into the next town of Itea. Here we were disgorged, still sleepy and bleary eyed, to await the Athens bus which called in on its way to Delphi. I must say the twenty mile journey up into the mountains soon blew away the cobwebs ... apart from the sheer beauty around us we were all petrified by the way the Greek coach driver nonchalantly hurtled his massive 60 seater coach round the endless mountain passes.

By 8.30 a.m. in the morning we had travelled nearly 30 miles from *Sanu* – and were in Delphi, that most holy of places in Greece, lying perched between earth and sky on the southern foothills of Mount Parnassus, with the limestone cliffs of the Phaedriades towering above. Once the site of the greatest oracle of the ancient world, Delphi is still one of the magical sights of our times, if only because of the splendour of its monuments and the grandeur of its scenery. The sacred grounds, surrounded by a wall, contain the ruins of a series of votive offerings, which various Greek cities presented to the God Apollo in commemoration of various important events. There are some twenty treasure houses in which are kept valuable trophies from wars, as well as a sanctuary, a small theatre, a palladium and the Temple of Apollo itself, which tends to dominate the whole area.

We spent a long day at Delphi, and none of us begrudged a minute of it, even though we were all thoroughly weary by the end of our climbings among the ruins. When we had finished with the mountainside we all went into the big museum with its priceless exhibits of archaic and classical sculptures – including the famous statue of the Charioteer. Our visit to the museum brought a touch of humour into an otherwise rather solemn occasion: the Greeks, sticklers for clothes etiquette, refused Llew entry into the museum because, although he was quite respectably dressed, he wore no shoes. This momentarily infuriated Frank and Kate, who had a big stand-up scene with the attendant: in the end honour was satisfied by Llew borrowing Frank's shoes for his visit.

As with our own private wedding, so it is equally difficult, I find, to capture the atmosphere of this more public occasion at Delphi. Even though by mid-day the place was positively teeming with visitors – Germans, Swedes, Danes, French, Italians, Japanese, you name the country, they were all there – somehow the underlying rather mysterious atmosphere was never completely lost. The setting really is so stupendous that it is not difficult to travel back in time and imagine all that went on, the ceremonies and the sacrifices, the solemn gatherings to hear the wisdom of the oracle. Would that our present day statesmen might take a leaf out of such primitive but perhaps wise ceremonies!

The day after we marvelled at the ancient magic of Delphi we were aboard *Sanu* sampling another of Greece's ancient wonders – the narrow 80 foot wide strip of the Corinth Canal. The history of this engineering feat goes back quite a time, and has an amazing precedent: *before* the canal was cut boats used to be hauled across the isthmus on rollers! There are, for instance, records of Augustus, after the Battle of Actium, having his ships dragged all the way across the land in pursuit of Antony. Proof of all this was supplied recently when excavations unearthed a section of a lime-stone-paved roadway, 14 feet wide and with two ruts, 5 feet apart, which bore the rollers. Even in those far off days the need for a canal was appreciated; it is recorded that the Roman Emperor Caligula had surveys made and that Nero even initiated some trial diggings, but they came to nothing. It was many centuries later, towards the end of the 19th century, in fact, that a French company finally completed cutting the canal's $3\frac{1}{4}$ miles length, most of it out of hard rock. It must have seemed an awesome task (in places the sides of the canal must be over two hundred feet deep) but one can see the attraction – the saving in distance by vessels proceeding to Piraeus from Brindisi, or vice versa, is almost 130 miles, compared to the outer route round the south tip of the Peloponnesus.

All this information I had swotted up before reaching the

canal. I had also taken due note of warnings that since vessels cannot pass one another in the canal they must wait outside until a blue burgee is hoisted to signify that the canal is clear and they may enter. In the Admiralty *Mediterranean Pilot Volume III* there was in fact a mass of rather formidable information: 'The Canal authority desire previous notice of intention to proceed ... the following particulars should be given; vessel's name, nationality, dimensions and net registered tonnage, ports of departure and destination, time of arrival, direction to proceed, if pilot or tug is required ... The vessel should have a ladder ready for the use of the Canal company's officials ... passage normally permitted by day or night, except Sunday, to vessels not more than 59 feet in beam, maxium draught of 23 feet, height of mast of 171 feet ... naval and mail vessels enjoy priority of tonnage ... vessels speed should not exceed 3 knots when entering the canal and 6 knots during transit' ... *and*, as a PS, 'with northern winds special care is required when entering the north western end of the canal.'

I kept re-reading that last line now as we approached the canal in a most troublesome and blustering wind, which was causing waves to race across the entrance to the canal. Would we be able to enter at all? I began to have some doubts as I saw two other big boats ahead of us sheer off, but decided to keep on – thankfully finding an easing of conditions once we got inside the initial area of entry.

In fact, our passage through proved a trouble-free one, the most out of the ordinary feature being the appearance of armed soldiers and machine gun posts at regular intervals along the canal bank – a sign of wartime precautions no doubt. At one point we had to pass under the lofty road and rail bridges, and cast rather nervous eyes upwards for we had heard horrific stories of children leaning over and dropping rocks to see if they could hit boats below! Fortunately they must have all been at school that day.

Our passage through the Corinth Canal seemed a memorable sort of occasion and we were just congratulating ourselves on apparently having made it entirely free of charge

– when a high powered motor launch came frothing up to us, hooting on its horn peremptorily. Coming alongside two officials jumped aboard, introduced themselves, took our particulars – and present me with a bill for about £10. Happily with one other exception, this was the only time during our Greek trip that, as a visiting yacht, we were required to pay any fees.

Curiously enough, that single other occasion followed almost immediately, upon our entering the nearby port of Piraeus and taking up a berth in Zea Marina, (Passalimani as it used to be known). Here we planned to spend nearly a week, taking the opportunity to pay several visits to nearby Athens, so we did not really feel it was unreasonable to have to pay a fairly modest charge for keeping our boat safely at a berth, with fresh water and electricity, groceries to the door and many other amenities. Zea Marina is in fact the largest harbour of its kind in Greece, a huge man-made marina which the Greeks organize most efficiently, with berths of about 600 boats at a series of pontoons and quays. Set in a huge bowl in the heart of Piraeus, surrounded (like its smaller companion-marina of Tourkolimano) by cafes and shops and cinemas, the Marina proved to be a lively and animated place, full of interest – not least, to us, in the variety of boats berthed there.

Indeed, for the first day or two we spent hours just wandering around the quays, looking at some of these boats: graceful schooners from the West Indies, majestic yachts from Italy and France and Sweden, huge steamers belonging to Greek millionaires and tiny ketches belonging to impoverished world yachtsmen – the variety was incredible, and fascinating. None of the boats were more romantic or beautiful, however, than the local Greek caique, with its high-pronged bow and colourful sails.

Unfortunately for us our arrival at Zea coincided with possibly the hottest spell of the whole summer in Greece, and with temperatures soaring up to nearly 100 degrees we all felt literally 'under the weather'. For the first time in my life I fell victim to heat exhaustion, being simply unable to move from my bunk for a whole day. Frank and Kate, too, were prostrate, and altogether this phenomenal heat did detract from the pleasure of our visit. Fortunately by evening the heat usually declined to more reasonable proportions, and it was then that we made our outings – to the Acropolis, to the marvellous National Museum, another evening wandering around the Plakka district, the Soho of Athens. Altogether we found Athens a remarkable and cosmopolitan city, full of interest.

Perhaps the time Jess and I saw it at its most wondrous was one evening when we got away on our own and caught the tiny funicular railway up to St. George's Monastery, an incredible mountain peak right in the centre of the city, from where, sitting at dinner in the unique restaurant perched on top, we had a grand stand view of the whole of Athens by night light. Not only was the view absolutely stupendous – so was the food, far and away the best meal of the whole trip. The reason, of course, was that it was French cooking, not Greek! We had long ago both come to the regretful conclusion that Greek cooking – served luke warm, swimming in fat, and very limited in choice – was not for us, hence our delighted surprise at our feast on top of St. George's.

Before leaving Malta for Greece I had made all kinds of complicated arrangements to have post delivered at Piraeus, but as is always the case on such occasions none of the letters we hoped for arrived, except a typical brusque note from Martin, back at Penzance, just to tell us that life was going along there all right. In particular we had no word from Demelza and her friend Diana, who were supposed to be waiting on the quay-side to join us for four weeks. The only thing to do was to make a long distance telephone call, which proved far less expensive and troublesome than I expected. In a few minutes I heard Demelza's excited familiar voice, assuring me that they had written (they had, to the wrong address) and repeating that they had been delayed, but were flying out that very next day and would get a taxi from the airport to the Marina.

At four o'clock the next day *Sanu* was already half way out of the Marina: we were all by now fed up with the closed-in heat, and only waiting to pick up our passengers before leaving for what we hoped would be the cooler climate of the islands. We had decided to get over the complicated business of hauling up our anchor and untying ropes, and now were just tied by a single rope to a large mooring buoy, with the dinghy lowered in readiness to fetch our new passengers. We had to wait nearly an hour and then we spied the taxi, disgorging Demelza and Diana and with what seemed an enormous amount of baggage (nearly all Diana's, one of these ladies who travels in style). Quickly Llew rowed over to the quay, loaded up the dinghy and brought them across ... there were a few hilarious moments of greetings and kisses, and then we were off, off in to the open sea again, thank goodness.

Typically the weather was quite rough for our ten mile crossing to the island of Aegina, where we anchored for the night, but then things calmed down in time for the next day's brief voyage to our real objective – this being the tiny Peloponnese harbour of Epidaurus. If the name strikes a faint bell, then this is as it should be, for Epidaurus is the name of one of the seven wonders of Greece – the site of the ancient amphitheatre, of that name, the best preserved theatre of its kind in the world. We had read about the theatre in some detail and I was determined to visit such an ancient site when it was in use – as it was every summer when performances of all the Greek classics were put on by distinguished actors and actresses for the National Theatre of Greece.

Now with our numbers swollen to eleven (and still two to come) we found we needed both dinghies to get ashore at Epidaurus. Awaiting us, and other visitors (many of whom came on ferries from Piraeus) were dozens of local taxis, so we hailed two and set off, on the twenty minute trip up into the mountains to our destination. Before we had travelled far we were joined by many other vehicles, taxis, private cars, motor coaches and local buses ... by the time we approached the theatre site we were reduced to one long traffic queue but once there everything seemed highly organised with huge parks for cars and coaches (there were literally dozens of the latter, most of them having brought parties from as far away as Athens, about a hundred miles distant).

We had, of course, swotted up the history of the theatre which is rightly regarded by the Greeks as one of their top tourist attractions, and we were expecting something pretty spectacular as we joined a seemingly endless column of fellow enthusiasts trudging up through the fragrant smelling pinewoods to the theatre itself (a column made up not merely of Greeks, but of French, Germans, Americans, Swedes, Danes, Italians, Japanese, Chinese – possibly every major nationality). When we reached the site our expectations were not disappointed!

Built in the fourth century BC by Polyolentus the Younger, Epidaurus is the best preserved theatre in Greece, capable of accommodating comfortably more than 14,000 spectators among its 55 tiers of stone seating. The vast amphi-theatre, set like a perfect bowl into the landscape, must be quite a stunning spectacle even when deserted and empty – when filled as it was on this night by a capacity audience the impact was even more breath-taking. Everywhere the eye was caught by a soothing colourful mass of movement – by contrast the centre-piece stage was outlined in lonely splendour by a single light.

At last all lights dimmed and the babel of conversations hushed as if by magic: off stage there was the sound of a horn blowing, we caught a first glimpse of white robed figures emerging from shadows – and we sat back relaxed, knowing that the performance had begun.

It was in fact, a performance of one of Greece's most famous classics, *Antigone*, a play peculiarly appropriate for a period when the whole country was in the throes of the renewed conflict with Turkey and the domestic upheavals of the eclipse of the infamous military junta, 'the Colonels'. Part of the play's theme is a plea for a more liberal way of life, a greater individual freedom – precisely what we gathered most Greeks were hoping for under their newly formed civilian government. Perhaps not surprisingly there were some electric moments during the play – as when after the princess had made an emotional and passionate speech about freedom, and proceedings were momentarily halted by a vast roar of enthusiasm from the preponderately Greek members of the audience.

The play itself was one of half a dozen Greek classics which make up the repertoire of the annual Epidaurus Festival, held every year during June and July and the early part of August. Sadly we had to confess that it was literally 'all Greek' to us since it was naturally performed in the native language. However, as with most of the world's masterpieces, something of the underlying and eternal verities comes through – and also we had with us Kate, who, as a drama producer, knew the play backwards, which at least made it easier for us to follow the action.

Not that there is much action in *Antigone*, at least on stage – most of it takes place conveniently off-stage and forms the subject of various impassioned speeches afterwards – nevertheless I think we all found the spectacle more gripping than we had anticipated. One reason for this was that we were privileged to watch first class theatrical performances by leading members of the National Theatre of Greece, from Athens: although many of them were highly paid stars they all regarded it as a great honour to be invited to act in such a revered setting. In the same way, the producers and set designers, even stage managers, were among Greek's finest.

Perhaps because of the language difficulties it is, indeed, the production side of *Antigone* which we remember most vividly – some most marvellous lighting effects, and the adroit use of the large chorus of white robed senators. Early in the play they walked impassively into the centre of the arena and then fanned out to form a large semi-circle, for most of the performance occupying this position of guardianship. Sometimes they chanted, other times individual members declaimed, or perhaps a few played solemnly on their instruments, flutes, pipes, cymbals ... whatever they did seemed to add an extra element of profundity to the proceedings.

In a potted biography of Epidaurus we had read an eulogy about the theatre's acoustic properties. You could, it was claimed, sit on the very top tier and still hear a pin drop on to the stage floor. Well, that might be an exaggeration, but only a slight one. During a tremulous hush in the play's action a cry from a baby in the audience sounded piercingly and almost deafeningly – at once there came an instinctive protesting hushing sound from the engrossed audience, and the unfortunate mother had to quickly depart with the offending infant. Of course she should never have brought such a tiny child in the first place – yet one can understand anyone's passionate eagerness to attend such a performance.

When it was all over and most of the leading characters had met their gory ends, when the great chorus at last turned and slowly padded away into the darkness, when all the lights had faded except for a solitary one illuminating the empty stage ... there was quite a long moment of stunned silence before the audience recovered to roar their final wild appreciation. I think everyone felt as we ourselves felt – overwhelmed by the sheer visual beauty and poignancy of the occasion. I remember we remained quite silent and thoughtful as we merged with the huge crowds and slowly wended our way back to our waiting taxi.

Later that night we all sat in *Sanu*'s stern in the little bay, under a shimmering silver moon. Stephen had his guitar, Genevieve brought out her silver flute, and with Demelza (the drummer of the family) tapping out an insistent beat with her hands on a small bonga, the rest of us were treated to half an hour of music, sometimes lifting our voices up and joining in some familiar chorus. It was a minor magic of our own to commemorate the major magic of earlier that evening – altogether an occasion we would long remember.

IX

Around the Cyclades Isles

When we sailed out of Epidaurus we left mainland Greece for the rest of our holiday and entered the fascinating, indeed unique world of the Greek Isles – those 'jewels of the Argan Sea' of which I, at any rate, had read so much, dreamed so much, and for so many years longed to visit. Now at last we were on our way, with a gay and lively crew to which we planned to add our last couple, our daughter Gill and her husband Alan, when we called at the northern-most island of Kea.

First, however, we paid a visit to Hydra, not strictly speaking a Cycladian island since it nestled fairly close in to the Peloponnese coastline. For some reason I had always had a pervasive conviction that I would like Hydra, which in all the photographs I had seen looked quite fascinating, especially the fish-bowl harbour with its tiers of white houses rising up all around – this, incidentally, was the island featured in an internationally successful Greek film, *The Woman in Black*. In the event, like most of my hunches this proved correct and we were all so delighted with Hydra that we stayed there nearly a week, wallowing in the island's attractive mixture of sophistication and solitude – quayside cafes reminiscent of the South of France combined with a law that no motor cars are allowed on the island, donkeys and mules being the only form of transport.

For all of us, I think, the main fascination of Hydra centred around its comparatively tiny little port into which, nevertheless, were packed the most impressive collection of yachts and schooners of all shapes and sizes. I had been forewarned about the harbour limitations, and my concern grew as we approached and I saw the inevitable forest of masts swaying in the afternoon breeze: I was much relieved when, upon entry, we saw a wide space ahead of us into which we should be able to tuck *Sanu*'s fat stern. Indeed I was much relieved that I managed to bring off one of our rare completely successful stern-to berthings, encouraged no doubt by the fact that there were several willing helpers along the quayside to take our ropes.

Once we were tied up we all flopped back and just revelled in the sights and sounds all around us. Few harbours can be so bright and colourful; not only are there the tall graceful masts of yachts lining the quayside, but in every direction the red roofed white houses rise up steeply as though forming a steep auditorium around a stage (the harbour). And then all along the quay there are the bright canopies of restaurants, open-air talbes and seats crowded with a variety of gaily dressed people ... here and there, rather incongruously, a passing 'train' of three or four donkeys, literally beasts of burden, carrying suitcases and sacks of potatoes and even (as we once saw) refrigerators and electric cookers.

Yes, we took to Hydra immediately. We liked especially, indeed found fascinating, the busy harbour life. Apart from the large Piraeus ferry boats that called in at least a dozen times a day, there were many local caiques edging up to the quay to land their loads of fresh vegetables and fruit brought over from the mainland. At Hydra's little market, incidentally, we had some of the best food of our whole trip. Oh, those huge and luscious peaches – what memories they bring back! And then there were the boats around us, such variety, so much beauty: and so constantly changing, that was another part of Hydra's attraction – during the daytime the harbour would be practically empty except for the trading caiques, then around five o'clock the first of the cruising yachts would come in, soon forming quite a queue. We were heartily glad we had made our entry in the early hours of the afternoon, for by six o'clock on most days there would not be a scrap of berthing space left. Woe betide a yacht that tried to come in later on – for, as the *Admiralty Pilot* puts it tersely, 'depths in the bay outside the breakwater are too great for anchorage' – and the only alternative was to sail away again to seek shelter elsewhere.

Many of the big yachts we found in Hydra were charter boats, that is to say elegant craft usually based on Piraeus, whose owners made a profitable income by taking passengers on summer cruises. Very often these owners remained ensconced in their wealthy homes in Athens and other comfortable spots, letting paid skippers do the donkey work. They certainly got a good return for their money. We were astounded at some of the sums being paid – sometimes as much as £200 a week per person (so that a yacht carrying six passengers was taking £1200 a week!). As always this sort of information prompted Jess to maintain that we should be doing the same with *Sanu*, but I had to point out to her that well-to-do-city types paying £200 a week would be hardly likely to appreciate the vagaries of *Sanu*'s very uncertain water system, or the erratic behaviour of her two hand-pumped flush toilets, not to mention a certain sparseness about some of her furnishings. Neither did we have any of the chrome-fitted showers and even bathrooms to be found on the luxury yachts. No, I said severely, nobody would put up with *Sanu* if they were paying really big money.

Mind you, we did come across a charter yacht which, while charging quite substantial fees, seemed to us very much a *Sanu* type of boat, both in the services it provided and the attitude of its crew. Needless to say we took a liking to this boat and the people on it! Stephen was particularly drawn to the pretty girl who was doing the cooking (causing some ructions with a watchful Gina!) and thanks to this interest, causing him to get friendly with the people on the boat, we came to know something about their set-up.

It was a nice old ketch, quite big, owned in partnership by two men, one of whom was aboard the boat as skipper, helped by a friend and by the girl. Although the boat was no doubt fundamentally sound it did seem plagued by troubles. There was a permanent leak in the stern gland ... the generator seldom worked ... the gears were often jammed ... and sometimes the water pump seized up. Thanks to Stephen's practical assistance some of these defects were remedied, but it became apparent to us that the people running the boat had very little time for their unfortunate paying guests. We could not help feeling sneakingly sorry for the latter, spying them sitting a little nervously at a table at the back of the boat on which were served up, rather peremptorily, breakfast consisting of a large box of Kellogg's Corn Flakes, some rolls and butter and a single jug of coffee. In the same spirit, if the water system was not working presumably the guests just had to do without washing. In some ways we had to admire the downright attitude of the boat owners, it made something of a pleasant contrast to the disgustingly servile attitude of so many of the crews of other charter boats. All the same, even on this yacht the passengers were paying about £60 a head a week!

Another boat whose crew we got talking to was a truly impressive miniature steamer, flying a German flag, whose skipper nonchalantly guided her with brilliant seamanship into a space about six inches wider than her beam. We were all truly impressed to find that the boat was so long and had so many crew members that they had to be equipped with walkie-talkie radios: the captain stood in his wheelhouse steering, with his radio close to his mouth, while two or three men hung over the back relaying information about how far the boat was off to the quay, etc. This struck us as the ultimate ploy – until someone told us of another boat which was fitted with two closed circuit television sets which enabled the captain to *watch* what was happening at his stern!

Fortunately the captain of the German boat – a Greek, as were most of the crews of the charter boats, no matter what their flags – proved friendly and amiable and spent quite a time chatting with us over a glass of ouzo. Apparently he worked busily from May to September, then retired to his home in Athens for a relaxed winter. Quite a nice life. His attitude to his passengers remained a little ambivalent as naturally he had to preserve discretion about his real opinions. We were troubled by no such inhibitions and in general found that the sort of people who paid £200 a week to travel about on charter boats were brittle and rather unattractive, using the boat merely as a convenient form of travelling, more interested in the social life of local night clubs and restaurants than the sea-going aspects. We used to watch them, dolled up to the eyebrows, as they tripped down their elegant gangplanks, looking very unnautical – and feel not a trace of envy.

During our stay at Hydra, egged on by our lively new arrivals, Demelza and Diana, our younger crew members took to visiting the local discotheque. In the process they generally imbibed sufficient local Greek wine to make their return journey, in the early hours of the morning a somewhat noisy affair. Lying awake in our cabin one night, Jess and I heard Demelza and Diana in the middle of a fearful quarrel, at the peak of which Diana flounced down to her cabin, packed her belongings into an enormous suitcase and lugged it up on deck announcing her intention of leaving forever.

Obviously feeling unable to make it across our open plank she planned to clamber aboard the adjoining German boat and get off on their safe gangway ... in the middle of all this, with Diana half across and Demelza trying to restrain her, there came a bloodcurdling scream. It turned out that Diana had dropped all her jewellery out of a handbag into the water! Jolly well serves her right, making such an awful din, we muttered turning over and trying to get to sleep. But Diana, resourceful as only as Australian can be, was up and out again next morning, at six a.m. having cajoled a slightly dazed Llewellyn (whom she had interrupted at his Yoga exercise) to start diving in the forlorn hope of retrieving her jewels. Not such a forlorn hope either, for Llew actually found every single item and kept appearing out of the water, spluttering and holding up each flashing object triumphantly.

I couldn't help smiling, remembering how Llew had earned my own undying gratitude at Syracuse when, leaning over the side to reach a dinghy, I saw my only pair of spectacles drop into some twenty feet of water. Fortunately they were in a case, and after diving five times Llew came up with the sodden package safely in his hand.

I suppose in many ways Hydra was not all that typical of the Greek Islands. It was comfortably off, quite luxurious, rather expensive, yet there was something very pleasant to me about the easy going café life, all literally at our stern. We had only to step off our plank and walk about six or seven paces to sink down into a comfortable seat, order a coffee or an iced orange or lemon drink – or maybe one of the scrumptious ice creams – and for the next couple of hours all we need do was sit back and watch the endless parade of people of all shapes and sizes, Greek, French, German, English, African, every sort of nationality, ranging from millionaire yacht owners to quite ordinary and generally likeable folk, like the three young Swedes we got talking to, who were going half way round the world in a tiny yacht about twenty feet long.

When tired of café life, it was interesting to browse among the gift shops with their quite fabulous selection of rugs and carpets and hand-woven dresses and ceramic jewellery and paintings and statues ... after which it would be time for a pleasant dip off the rocks at the southern end of the harbour, within sight of the nearby mainland shores.

When finally we returned to *Sanu* to eat bread and cheese and fruit up on the deck we could then watch one or other of the inevitable ready-made entertainments that always seemed to be taking place – such as the arrival of one of the big ferry boats, say the *Mykonos*. This particular boat gave us a good laugh; its captain must have been something of a 'whiter than white' perfectionist, for hardly was she tied up when two or the crew were sent along the quayside with long poled brushes, buckets and tins of paint. First they would laboriously scrape away any signs of dirt around the opening where the anchor chain rattled down to the water (and of course every time the anchor was pulled up in brought its share of mud and dirt). Next the two men would gravely wash down a large area of white around the hole ... and finally, in case there were any unseemly scratches or other marks, they changed to paint brushes and very carefully painted over any offending patches.

Another perpetual source of interest was the huge water boat which came over from Poros every day. The first time we saw this boat approaching we could hardly believe our eyes: its decks were awash, actually under the sea it seemed, and only its superstructure at the stern travelled above water. Was she sinking? Making a last desperate try to reach harbour? No, none of these things. She was simply laden to the brim with a fresh water supply for Hydra – an island which, despite its name, is completely waterless and entirely dependent on the daily trips of the water boat. Usually the water boat would tie up at a special point further up the harbour where hose pipes were connected to pump the water out into huge storage tanks – we always enjoyed watching the miraculous conversion from a semi submarine into a normal, quite large cargo carrying boat, as the boat rose higher and higher out of the water. When it was completely empty the captain and his two men crew would start up the engine then reverse into a berth alongside *Sanu*, where she remained overnight until about 5 a.m., then off she went to get the next day's supply, and so on.

Yes, there was always plenty going on in Hydra. One day I had violent toothache and embarked on a Kafka-like quest through winding alleyways, desperately searching for a dentist I could not quite believe existed. In fact, he did, was very professional, spoke no English but enough French for us to communicate – and within five minutes had whipped out the offending molar.

Another day it was Jess's turn to quest. looking for one of the wooden donkey saddles she had noticed were used by all the Hydra muleteers. As with the dentist, so her quest was successful: one day a grinning Jess came along followed by a sweating fat muleteer carrying in his portly arms one of the huge and very cumbersome donkey saddles. I ought to have taken warning from the fact that its awkward shape would not allow it to gain entry into any of the cabins, and we had eventually to lower it by rope through the skylight of the aft cabin. (The reader can imagine our later experiences on buses and trains).

'How much?' I said grimly.

'Twelve pounds,' said Jess, almost ecstatically. 'Isn't it a bargain?'

I groaned. 'I only hope Esmeralda will think so!'

Yes, indeed, we thoroughly enjoyed our stay at Hydra – and were quite sorry when our timetable necessitated leaving for the northern Cycladian island of Kea, where we had arranged to meet Gill and Alan. As it happened we very nearly did not leave. When we came to start the engine we found the magneto out of order, and Stephen and Llewellyn had to spend five hours down in the oily dungeon of the engine room before finally, just after lunch, the engine roared into life. By then I was a little worried about the time element, for it was forty miles to Kea, and I didn't want us to arrive there after dark ... however I decided we ought to just about make it.

Later that afternoon, or rather early evening, as dusk began to make warning signals of arriving and we were only just beginning to approach Kea, quite a long island, my nervousness returned. According to Captain Denham Kea had only one good harbour, St. Nikolaos on the north west tip, and this was what we were looking for – but could we spy the opening? We went in quite close to the rather barren looking land, and ticked off one small inlet after another without coming upon the one which we knew we would immediately recognise because it would reveal Kea's only lighthouse. Darker and darker grew the surrounding clouds, the sea was whipping up, I did not like the look of things at all ... What on earth would we do if we just never found the opening? Then, thankfully, we rounded a sharp point and there was the lighthouse we had wanted. Akra Ayfou Nikolao a square tower on an octagonal base. Soon we had passed into a large and sheltered bay and were anchoring off the tiny village of Vourkari. Peace at last.

Unfortunately peace was not a quality I found at Kea. However most of the others quite took to this rather sparsely populated island (later it was to attain notoriety as the place selected for the exile of the Greek colonels), and there was quite an expedition of them on the long bus journey up into the mountains to visit the capital town and especially to inspect the famous local celebrity, a large 40 foot lion in base relief cut into the face of a rock. I contented myself with filling *Sanu* up with water from a well at Vourkari, an operation involving us in borrowing 200 feet of hose from a neighbouring yacht as the depths at the quay were too shallow for *Sanu* and we had to anchor some way out. For a cost of £1 we got 400 gallons of lovely fresh Greek spring water – just as well, too, as several of the crew who were not used to being waterless had got near mutiny point.

No, as far as I was concerned, I got bad 'vibs' at Kea, and was only waiting for the arrival of Gill and Alan on the ferry from Lovrion. Alas, for two days they just never arrived, and we were getting really worried when finally they made a welcome appearance. They had left their luggage at the nearby port of Livadhi, where the ferry had called, and walked along the coastroad to our anchorage, so later on Stephen and Alan went off in the small Campari to fetch the suitcases. To our surprise they returned rather mysteriously two hours later by taxi – bearing in their arms not merely the luggage but the bedraggled remains of the Campari. Landing in the dark they had run against a sharp iron spike which had punctured the inflatable, and they had only with difficulty saved the boat and outboard engine. Ah well, perhaps that was what I had felt my vibs about!

It was good to be off early the next morning – until we got out of the shelter of our bay and found a full-scale meltemi blowing, a wind of at least Force 6, maybe Force 7. We were to discover from now on that the Meltemi would almost always be with us – a North West wind that blows from mid-July right through to mid-September in the Aegean Sea – and there was nothing to do but make the best of it. On that initial occasion I have to admit my mind played with the idea of turning back to nearby shelter. I shelved such unworthy thoughts when Alan and Gill said airily it had been much rougher coming over on the ferry.

In the event we had quite an exhilarating sail across the thirty miles to our destination of Siros. The wàves were coming across us so that *Sanu* got a good deal of rolling from side to side, but after a while we got used to the motion. Llewellyn in particular was delighted. He had been demanding a spell of rough weather for some time, and now he had it. Despite our warning he went and sat right in the bows, frequently being soaked by spray, and grinning all over his now bronzed face.

It was certainly a boisterous sort of trip, and I can't say I was sorry when at last we turned into Siros harbour, a large commercial harbour lined with quite sizeable boatyards and slips, and even possessing a huge dry dock. We were pretty tired after the buffeting of our trip and it was with relief that I saw a wide quay ahead of us, only sparsely populated by three or four yachts. Shouldn't be much problem berthing there. ...

Half an hour later I was ruefully regretting such false optimism, and we were in the middle of one of those ridiculous crises that every now and then spring up over our berthing. When Llew came to try and row ashore with the ropes he found such a strong wind blowing off the shore that he simply could not make any headway. In desperation he sculled back to the boat and Alan joined him to lend power to the rowing. Alas, not even two pulling with all their strength could get the dinghy any nearer to the shore. Needless to say the usual crowd of delighted onlookers had gathered, now and then giving encouraging cheers which made Alan and Llew blush crimson with annoyance. Meantime aboard *Sanu* we had dropped our anchor and could do nothing except meander backwards and forwards, or just drift. What on earth were we going to do?

We were just debating the next move when a young man off one of the yachts nonchalantly dived into the water, swam out to us and called out, 'Why not give me the rope and I'll swim ashore with it?' I am ashamed to say that this simple expedient had never occurred to me, but ever since then it has become our standard practice, for of course it is much easier for one man to slip through the water than struggle with an inflatable.

Now followed one of those coincidences that do so much to enliven cruising. The young man who helped us, Nigel, was crewing on a small Hillyard yacht whose owner, Chris, turned out to be someone we had met three years previously when we had all been winter berthing at Monsieur Palumbo's boatyard at Agde, up the River Herault in Southern France. Since then Chris and his wife, with help occasionally from friends such as Nigel, had been wandering all over the Mediterranean, much further afield than we had yet managed. We had much to talk about regarding our various adventures – including the sobering fact that only that day Chris had been quoted 7000 drachmas (nearly £100) for slipping his quite small yacht. (Feeling sorry for him then I was soon to feel much sorrier for myself when on inquiry at Perama, near Piraeus, I was quoted 15,000 drachmas, that is more than £200 just to slip *Sanu*!)

We didn't stay long at Siros, as we were anxious to make the two hour crossing to the legendary island of Delos, one-time capital of the Cyclades. Once again magneto trouble held us up for several hours, and once again we only just managed to find our haven before darkness – this time Fourni Bay, a tiny indent in the coastline of Delos which had been recommended by Captain Denham as 'safe and comfortable especially during Meltemi conditions'. Perhaps things were worse than usual; at any rate we found precious little shelter and though we put out over a hundred foot of chain in about sixteen feet of water we had the greatest misgivings about *Sanu*'s safety. By now it was dark and we were surrounded on all sides by rocks and barren cliffs, so we decided to do something unusual for us, to mount an anchor watch. This meant dividing into couples, and spending an hour each couple on guard during the night, peering anxiously around to make sure that the land was not moving, which would have indicated anchor dragging. It was altogether a worrying time.

The next day we had our recompense. Legend has it that

Delos, about three miles long and a mile across, floated around in the Aegean sea until Leto, pregnant by Zeus, took refuge on the island after being denied shelter elsewhere because people feared the wrath of Hero, Zeùs's jealous wife. Leto was allowed to stay on Delos only after pledging that her children would recognise the island as his or her birthplace and dwell there forever – in due course Leto gave birth to Apollo, worshipped by the ancients as the God of Light and Music, and his twin sister, Artemis, Goddess of Hunting.

Delos's glory, however, rests on a great deal more than mere legend. Excavations on Mount Cynthus have shown that the island was known to the pre-Hellenic tribes of the Mediterranean and famed among the Minoan Cretans as long ago as 3000 B.C. In Mycenaean times it was a trading centre and important port, used by early seafarers as a transition stop for travelling from Europe to the Orient. Later it became a famous religious centre, with many temples and other edifices, acquiring fabulous treasures (many of which were stolen by the rulers of Athens and stored on the Acropolis). In 314 B.C. Delos obtained its freedom and for the next two hundred years flourished again as a great trading centre, with wealthy merchants building luxurious villas on the island. More temples were erected, almost many new shrines and sanctuaries, and an impressive protective wall was built around the town.

Alas, with the coming of Christianity Apollo lost his following, the pilgrimages dwindled, and suddenly the peoples of Delos found themselves unable to earn a living and were forced to move to more prosperous areas. Before long temples and monuments and even tombs were torn down, either by plundering pirates or by ignorant neighbouring islanders seeking materials with which to build their cottages. Delos, the fabled ancient capital of the Cyclades, faded into history.

Fortunately, as we were now to discover, thanks to years of patient work and excavations by scholars of Hellonic history, from out of history has emerged Delos, 'the Pompeii of the Aegean'. Only in Pompeii, indeed, had we seen such a profusion of a preserved civilisation, ranging from ancient temples to palladiums, from an amphitheatre to a shopping street, from the smallest house to the grandest villa.

During our long and magical day at Delos we saw most of these ruins. First we landed by dinghy at a small white sandy beach, then we followed a goat track across stony fields which eventually brought us to the first of several temples whose pillars reared up impressively against the skyline. In one of these, heavily guarded by iron railings to protect them from possible vandalism, we found a series of marvellously preserved coloured mosaics – one showing Dionysius riding a panther, another a pair of dolphins.

Next we visited the House of Hermes, built during the Hellenistic period, its three storeys showing the prosperity and riches of the inhabitants of that time: then after a look at Apollo's Sanctuary, on to the Temple of Hercules, a strange structure built into a deep crevice within the rock, its roof made of granite rafters in early Hellenistic times. Here we ate our picnic lunch before following the custom of islanders three thousand years ago and climbing to the top of Mount Cynthus along an ancient track whose steps are hewn out of the rock.

From the top of Mount Cynthus, buffetted by relentless winds so strong that we leaned against them without falling down, there was the reward of a fabulous panoramatic view over the whole of Delos and across to Rhenia in the west and Mykonos in the north east. In many ways I think this was a supreme moment of the visit, for at such a height, and with such an all round view, we really captured the full flavour of ancient Delos.

Even so we were suitably awed and impressed when we walked down again, round the rim of the ancient open air theatre, and then following the cobbled steps of what had once been the main shopping street of a bustling market town, lined on either side by quite recognisable ruins of houses, shops and meeting places, many with inner courtyards and colonnaded verandahs and here and there the remnants of marble tables and terra cotta stoves. Just as in Pompeii it required very little effort of imagination to conjure up quite vivid images of 'life in the old days', when the little streets had been alive with bustling figures hurrying about on their affairs.

At its end the cobbled main street broadened out into what had once been the town square, and then led down to the original ancient jetty of the port, where in olden times many proud sailing ships had been moored. Today there is a more modern jetty built alongside, and to this very day caiques from Mykonos bring over large numbers of tourists. Some of these were now embarking for the return journey, and as the graceful caique motored away towards the northend of the straits it was again not very difficult to take our minds into the past and imagine we were watching some heavily laden trading schooner embarking for Piraeus.

Our tour of Delos was nearly over – but not quite. There was still the small but fascinating museum, with its varied collection of pottery and jewellery and other items found on the island. Beside the museum, very sensibly, the Greek Tourist Board has established a small café where the hot and weary visitors (as by then we were!) can obtain the marvellous modern invention of refrigerated cold drinks, and ice creams.

Suitably refreshed we were on our way back when we had our last unexpected delight – coming across the astonishing sight of five great white lions standing eternal guard over Delos town. These were of course not real lions, but archaic lions sculptured out of marble as long ago as the year 700 B.C., and presented to the people of Delos by the inhabitants of neighbouring Naxos, where the marble is still mined. Symbols of immense power and superiority the lions (originally there were more, but still five stand in full splendour) are rather charmingly described in the official guidebook as 'poised to watch straight ahead, they bedeck the flank of the terrace leading to the holy lake: sleepless sentinels of the Sacred Precinct for 25 centuries now!'

We wended our way back to our boat by walking along the very edge of the shore – even here there were the ruins of dwellings right down to the lapping waves, and often we stepped over broken pots and other remnants. When we got back to the sandy beach the invitation of the crystal clear water was irresistible, and we all enjoyed a cool swim before rowing over to *Sanu*. That evening, to round off an unforgettable day, we ate our supper on deck under the benevolent light of an almost full moon, while all around us mysterious memories of past centuries stirred and whispered. Truly a day to remember – our dreamy day at Delos.

X

A Visit to Atlantis

From Delos to Mykonos is only about five miles but when we set off the next morning on this very short journey we found ourselves going from one world to another – in more senses than one. The first problem was the arrival of a full scale Meltemi wind, far stronger than anything we had encountered previously on our trip. Leaving Delos by the North channel meant heading straight into the wind, and what was worse coping with the freak conditions produced by a passage through a narrow strait, with rocky shallows on either side (for those nautically innocent, the net result is to create much larger and more dangerous waves than would have been the case in open sea).

For a couple of miles *Sanu* was bucking up and down like a bronco steed – some of these short sharp waves must have been more than twenty feet high. We were all quite petrified: firstly at some of the almost perpendicular rise and falls, secondly at the knowledge that depths below us, even though officially thirty feet or so, could mean we might even touch bottom in one of those violent troughs. Fortunately we survived (thank heaven we did not have to make a sharp turn in such conditions, I fancy then even *Sanu* might have rolled over) and headed hopefully towards our next harbour at Mykonos.

Here we encountered the second major problem. Rather like Corfu earlier in the trip, Mykonos harbour apparently had been designed by a sadist who had provided some sort of shelter in other directions, but little or no shelter against the one prevailing north-west wind. As a result even after we had passed between the two harbour breakwaters and were within a hundred feet or so of rows of packed boats – even then the wind was blowing in with full force.

What made matters worse was that, as *Sanu* continued to buck about and we looked around desperately, it became self evident that to paraphrase a famous saying, there was 'No Room at the Inn'. Literally: every available inch of space in the town part of the harbour was occupied by local caiques and fishing boats, while over in the north corner the derisory 'Yacht Harbour', which consisted of about fifty feet of poorly sheltered quay, was completely occupied by a row of half a dozen yachts – and even they looked most uncomfortable, tossing all over the place. It began to seem as if we had entered some sort of nautical inferno; gone were all our fond hopes of leisurely tying up and having a mid-morning cup of coffee – we were in trouble, we had nowhere to moor.

In the end we did the only remaining practical thing, we went alongside a big gravel-carrying steamer tied up at the outer edge of the north quay. Not only was this a very exposed position but a doubly uncomfortable one, as we were promptly to discover, for on the other side of the gravel boat a whole section of the quay's protective wall had been ripped away by past meltemis, allowing a permanent semi-hurricane wind to blow right across the gravel boat. Since all day long cranes were emptying grab loads of gravel from the boat into waiting lorries the unpleasant result can be imagined: in no time at all *Sanu* was covered from head to foot in a thick coat of gravel dust. It coated the deck, it clung to the sides and doors, it obliterated the view and light from all the windows, in short it almost choked up our whole existence.

On top of all this inconvenience the only way we could get on or off *Sanu* was by some acrobatic climbing across decks of the gravel boat, with a final horrific jump on to the quay beyond – and even then we had to chose the right moment to avoid being pulverised by the swinging grab arms!

Not surprisingly everyone was up in arms, tending to blame

the captain, but when I gestured around and asked what was the alternative, no one had an answer. The sad fact was that the wind continued to blow without respite for the next five days, and for the next five days we simply had to remain at our uncomfortable 'berth'. Such was our unhappy introduction to Mykonos, the most popular, cosmopolitan and architecturally attractive of all the Cyclades Isles – the St. Ives of Greece, as we quickly decided from our knowledge of that very similar Cornish fishing village-cum-holiday resort. Here I cannot resist quoting, rather ruefully, from an official publication.

Visitors to Mykonos soon find themselves caught up in the whirlwind of island life – perpetually on the move like one of her 365 graceful wind-mills. Daybreak is a magical time: the sun slowly rises, revealing one layer of white after another from the shadows, finally emerging in all its golden splendour from behind the mountain. In the daytime long stretches of unspoiled beaches await the dedicated swimmer. A fish-filled rocky underwater world awaits the keen harpoonist, while water-skiing attracts the adventurous. Other delights include countless little tavernas, marvellous scenery wherever you walk, night clubs which stay open around the clock – and the Pelican of Mykonos wandering casually among new and familiar faces.

Well, it's all true enough, including the Pelican (except that we found *three* wandering about, not just one, so business must be brisk!) but the fact is that Mykonos would have had to be quite superlative in its attractions to have compensated for our uncomfortable berth. As it was we *did* enjoy wandering up and down the winding alleyways – so like St. Ives, with little gift shops and restaurants tucked away in the most unlikely nooks and corners – and we *did* love the columns of white houses, the dramatic wind-mills, the equally dramatic little white chapels – and we *did* enjoy several pleasant outings to golden sandy beaches including 'Paradise Beach', where nude bathing was officially allowed. We were not so happy about a 'grand' meal out which ran up a bill of £25 including £5 for a single lobster, and we were plagued by technical problems such as the lack of any fresh water supply, and the inability to find anyone willing to bring a supply of diesel oil up to *Sanu*. Add to that the fact that the whole town, beautiful though it was, was almost swamped by armies of backpackers and – well, you will get the general idea that our visit was hardly an unqualified success.

Matters were not helped when we discovered that our magneto had packed up again, this time more seriously. Poor Stephen and Llewellyn, with the assistance of a willing Alan, spent hours and hours struggling to repair the damage, taking the mechanism to pieces, putting it together again, realigning the timing of the main engine, patiently going through a whole series of procedures. Up in the wheel-house I would move about uneasily, aware that for the want of this one tiny item, the mighty *Sanu* might just as well be on dry land, she would not move another foot. It would have taken weeks to have had a replacement brought out from England, even if one had been available. Oh, what a relief when at long last the boys came up, oily but triumphant, thumbs confidently in the air. And, fingers crossed, it worked adequately from that moment right through to nearly the end of the trip – and even then it half worked enough to get us back to Piraeus.

It was very noble of Llew to spend those last two days working on the magneto, for in fact he and Frank and Kate, and little Nell, were all due to leave us at Mykonos, catching one of the big ferry boats back to Piraeus and a fearsome train journey across Europe to England. Somehow this was typical of Llewellyn, a sweet natured fellow who is always willing and helpful, the ideal member of a boat crew. We were sorry to see him and the others making their final preparations, packing away presents and so forth, finally embarking at eight o'clock in the morning on the voyage to Piraeus. Owing to the seemingly perpetual winds, the ferry boat was not able to come into the harbour but anchored across the mouth, passengers being taken out in little caiques. When Llew, Frank, Kate and Nell were aboard the ferry they lined the deck and waved to us rather forlornly … a sad, sad moment.

After Mykonos, our next port of call, Naxos, was a great relief. Here, at what is the largest and most mountainous of all the Cyclades Isles, we found complete shelter, a ready supply of fresh water, an equally ready supply of diesel fuel – and to cap it all, the enjoyable company of an old friend from earlier cruising days.

This was that remarkable old man Charles Rayner whom we found snugly tucked away in a corner of the harbour in his small Harrison sloop in which this intrepid septuagenarian spends his leisurely life wandering around the Mediterranean. I have described in *Spring at Land's End* our first encounter with Charles then in the small Corsican port of Calvi, and how he finally set sail for Italy and unknown shores. Well for the past year or so he had been haunting the Greek Isles, having, like us all, fallen in love with their variety and richness of scenery, and was now on his way back to his base port of Spetsai, where he berthed for the winter. Now he had much to talk about over a lively meal down in *Sanu*'s saloon, with no fewer than ten of us round the long table. For most of the trip of course, we used to eat out on deck, but this night it was a bit cold and it was cosy and friendly to gather in the saloon and toast Charles's health in Samos wine (the best in Greece we found).

We were glad of Charles's company in more senses than one, for on our second day, when Stephen and Alan had gone off to climb a mountain, I was suddenly told I must move *Sanu* further along the quay to make room for a big ferry. Fortunately Charles was friendly with the owner of a nearby MFV type of boat (built of ferro-concrete) and with the aid of this good soul to operate my anchor winch, and Charles going along the quay, we managed the right manoeuvres. I must say I enjoyed the look on Stephen and Alan's faces when they came back from their mountain trip!

The next day we went our separate ways, Charles bound for Paros and ourselves heading for Ios, one of the lesser known islands, about which Ernle Bradford had written ecstatically in his book, *The Greek Isles*. Here we anchored in the middle of a beautiful bay known as 'Little Malta', with mountains rearing around in all directions, an extremely sheltered anchorage, and wallowed in the lazy indolent life which is part of the *raison d'être* of cruising – swimming off the side of the boat, rowing ashore to sunbathe on white sands, taking turns to watch through the binoculars what was going on ashore, or maybe to follow the tinkling progress of a herd of mountain goats. Here, too, we celebrated Demelza's 23rd birthday, rather magically, sitting in an open air restaurant on the water's edge with *Sanu* riding in the centre of the bay flooded by moonlight. Because it was getting late in the season the restaurant was empty except for our party, and the owners charmingly made up a bouquet for Demelza and generally added to the festivity of the occasion.

Sitting back and smiling indulgently at the happy family scene Jess and I could not help remembering that when we first got *Sanu* Demelza had still been a small schoolgirl of thirteen. How quickly the ten years had passed – but yet, to be honest, how much had been accomplished. Aboard our faithful old boat we had sailed not merely the seventeen miles to Mevagissey (the very first trip on our own) – but also the 3,000 miles to Denmark and Sweden and back again: not only the 40 short but dangerous miles to the Isles of Scilly, but the 2,000 long and even more dangerous miles around the Atlantic coast of Spain and Portugal, and into the Med. And after that – Ibiza, Majorca, the South of France, Elba, Corsica, Sardinia, Italy, Malta. It all sounded rather like extracts from a package-tour brochure, but had been so much more interesting because, to quote Mr Sinatra, we had done it our way.

And of course not least of the pleasures of doing it our way has been the opportunity it affords to have together, brief though it may be, most of the family. We are all scattered now, but we have come to value these reunions greatly. It is a great delight to welcome loved and familiar faces aboard dear old *Sanu*. And equally a great sadness when we have to say goodbye, as now, at Ios, we had to say goodbye to Demelza and Diana. We had thoroughly enjoyed their stay, for they had brought a gust of new life with them. This time they did not leave us: we sailed away in *Sanu* leaving the two girls standing all lonely and lost on the quayside, as their ferry had been delayed.

At last we were heading for the most southern of our destinations – and indeed the high peak of our trip – a long planned visit to the island of Santorini, or Thira, reputedly the famous long lost island of Atlantis. Experts may still argue about the exact location of this legendary place, but as you approach Santorini – through a fantastic bay, the crater of a volcano, bounded by the islands of Aspronisi and Therasia, with cliffs rising sheer out of the water to a height of nearly 1000 feet – puny mortal doubts seem to dwindle. Sailing across this indigo blue sea-in-a-crater (depths 1200 feet and more), part of it still smouldering, we all sensed that the majestic scenery around us had been created by strange and almost incomprehensible forces. It was quite literally out of this world.

Historically the facts are simple enough. Some 3,500 years ago Santorini was a single mountainous mass, almost completely round, and inhabited by a highly sophisticated race of people enjoying (as has been shown clearly by archaeological finds) a civilisation that was dazzling and delightful – but, alas, also doomed. What put an end to the island's glowing prospects was a single but tremendous volcanic eruption of quite unprecedented violence, followed by the collapse of the whole centre of the island, an area of some fifty square miles: the sea rushed into the immense lava pool, setting up gigantic hundred foot high waves which swept away to destroy large areas around the Aegean Sea, among them the palaces of Minoan Crete, some sixty miles away (there are reliable records that the tidal wave was still thirty feet high when it reached Egypt). Santorini itself was totally covered in volcanic ash, in places to a depth of 150 feet, thus erasing a rich and powerful state.

Much of this we had read about before our arrival, yet the physical impact remained as startling as ever. Entering the wide sheltered strait we were surrounded on all sides by the most amazingly sheer cliffs (once the interior of the crater) whose sides looked rather like a cake sliced into half – the colours ash red and black, splattered with white limestone, often corrugated as if with pillars, and sometimes dotted by caves. Equally dramatic were the four or five brilliant white townships perched on the very cliff-tops and forming a broad white ribbon on the skyline – most prominent among them the capital, Thira, whose striking buildings included both a modern cathedral and an old Greek Orthodox Church.

Our anchorage, in fact, was directly below Thira, though anchorage is hardly the correct word: in fact at depths of more than 1200 feet no boats can anchor but have to make use of several strong buoys which have been permanently moored just off a small quayside. We tied up to one of these buoys and then rowed ashore in our dinghy to make the first of several somewhat hair raising journeys by mules up a mule track which zig zags up the 700 foot precipitous slope. In the words of a local guide 'these beasts are in good supply and the muleteers make a lucrative trade carrying tourists up and down between the landing and Thira.' You can say that again – our first asking price was 60 drachmas, or nearly £1! However, forewarned, we bargained, and as during the ensuing week we became regular travellers, managed to get the price down to a much more reasonable 25 drachmas. Even so none of us fancied the ride down, with the mules slipping all over the place in their own excrement (curiously although this was left to rot on the cobbles there was practically no odour) and the land appearing to fall away from below our very feet.

The view from the top – after we had with some difficulty picked our way through a steep cluster of touristy gift shops overflowing with hand-made rugs, jewellery, pottery and wines, all locally made (and the wine, at least, excellent value, branded perhaps not surprisingly 'Atlantis') – was pretty spectacular. Across the other side of the deep waters were high cliffs – in the middle, sticking out like some blackened sore thumb, 'the Burnt Isles', the Kemmeni lava islets, some of which have only made their appearance quite recently. The largest (438 feet) erupted out of the water in 1707, and is a solid mass of lava and cinders which in 1943, that is not much more than 30 years ago, erupted further, forming a second island. We could not help feeling a little uneasy as we learned that some form of disturbance was to be expected roughly every 25-30 years ... after all, describing one of these eruptions in the year 200 BC, a local scribe had left an alarming account of how 'flames rushed forth from the sea for a space of four days, causing the whole of it to boil and be on fire'.

Fortunately nothing like this happened the day we crossed by dinghy to land at a small rough quay built at the head of a small cove where sulphur fumes still spewed out into the sea bed (local fishermen, we learned, take advantage of this natural benefit by anchoring their caiques in the cove for several days, thus ensuring a natural anti-fouling by the sulphur). From the moment we set foot on the curiously arid and barren landscape we all felt the same profound sense of unease. This was not a normal landscape, but a mass of tangled twisted lumps of blackened rock, some of it forming quite agonised shapes.

When we reached the lip of what we thought might be one vast crater we found that instead there were several smaller ones, many of them still smoking and smouldering. Everywhere there was such a sense of awful desolation – nothing growing, no birds, no life – that we were quite glad to return to the quay and set off back to our floating home. Indeed we were even glad that one of the regular cruise liners had tied up on one of the other buoys, all a blaze of bright life and laughter – quite a relief after such desolation.

Later we mingled among many hundreds of tourists – Americans and Germans in preponderance – whose regular presence helps towards a pretty healthy local economy, able to support a population of more than 15,000 (next to tourism, wine producing and pumice mining are the main industries). When the cruise boats are in Santorini's weirdly beautiful capital town teems with life, and has much to offer – a fascinating museum, several crafts centres, a carpet factory, a cathedral – as well as more sophisticated pleasures, discotheques, night clubs, hotels, shops with English newspapers. Then there are excellent and cheap bus services around the island to the other attractions – notably several beautiful long beaches, such as Kamari, five miles unbroken stretch of beautiful *black* sands.

One day some of us followed an old goat track up to the highest point on the island, Korif Ayies Ilias, to give it the Greek name, a conical peak nearly 2000 feet high on the summit of which was our objective, a remarkable white square monastery which at a distance even more impressive in olden days but now the Greek Government has built beside it an enormously powerful strategic television aerial, and military and monks live side by side. Our visit was purely to the Monastery of Ilias, however, and at first there was some horror at our appearance wearing shorts and singlets (after all the temperature was over 90 degrees!). Fortunately the tubby little monk in charge decided to make a compromise, opened a cupboard and brought out several robes and wound them round our indecently exposed bodies. Thus attired we had a fascinating tour not only of beautiful chapels and so on, but also of the monks' pottery and wine making centres, also a library full of precious old manuscripts. After a welcome glass of home made black-currant juice we were sent on our way along an incredibly beautiful mountain path which brought us eventually to the ancient city of Thira, a kind of miniature Pompeii, 2000 feet up for safety.

All this was interesting enough but the peak of our visit was still to come. We had heard many rumours of the excavations started in 1967 by Professer Marinates, Director of the Greek Department of Antiquities, which have revealed the ruins of a considerable Minoan township which had lain buried for some 3,500 years. These excavations were centred on a site near the village of Akrotiri on the South side of the island, so now we sailed round and anchored in a sheltered bay within sight of the huge protective dome under which the excavations were going on. We rowed ashore and filed into the site, being at once caught up with the feeling of excitement which must come to anyone seeing 'work in progress' on an archaeological site. Here were the rooms of houses actually half exposed – tables still strewn with everyday pots – water pitchers still standing in what would have been the kitchen – mosaics, or traces of them, still colourfully adorning walls. What is gradually emerging is of vast importance, a relic of when Minoan civilisation was at its peak, a township complete with buildings standing two and three stories high and remnants of balconies, squares, shops, workshops, places of worship (it is from these that recently the Greeks have taken the marvellous frescoes now installed in a special room at the National Museum in Athens – 'The Two Antelopes'. 'The Boy Boxers' and 'The Blue Monkeys'). These works are remarkable for their consummate artistic perfection – and so, we were assured, is the greatest discovery of all, still in process of being re-assembled, a frescoe which covers three walls and unfolds from left to right, and comprises eighty men and women, some twenty ships, at least three towns and some exotic landscapes. Professor Marinates regards it as 'a composition unique for its totality and without any doubt whatsoever constituting the most important historical monument of the Aegean Bronze Age.'

Not surprisingly we found it hard to leave Santorini! Even after the excavations we did no more than turn round and sail back to our friendly buoy off Thira, determined to enjoy a last magical night – marvelling at the stupendously beautiful scenery, the cliffs invested, at sunset, with all kinds of improbable colours. Yes, indeed, Santorini was the experience of a lifetime, and never to be forgotten.

XI
Meltemi Madness

After Santorini the truly traumatic period of our cruise began – or shall I say, more simply, the meltemi struck! As I have hinted once or twice this north west wind (sometimes veering north east, but always generally from the north) seemed determined to interfere with our leisurely progress. Despite having read constant warnings in the text books about the meltemi I must confess I had not taken it very seriously ... and indeed even on some of those earlier occasions, as on the trip from Kea to Siros or at Mykonos, though the wind had been infuriating it had never seemed really dangerous. Perhaps I had grown too complacent: at any rate during the last two weeks of our voyage I was to be taught several sharp salutary lessons about life on the ocean waves.

The first of these took place at one of the most idyllic anchorage of our whole trip, a most beautiful spot, Port Vathy, on the small and less well known island of Siphnos, a secluded land-locked bay into which we found our delighted way late one evening after a calm and perfect sail from Santorini. When we awoke the next morning it was like being in a minor paradise, lush mountains rearing in the background and a vast white sandy beach almost encircling us – ashore glimpses of white-washed cottages and a typical Greek taverna with its bamboo roof. The sun was shining brightly in a perfect blue sky, we could smell fragrant pinewood scents from distant woods – why, we could hardly wait to get ashore and explore. Besides, we had a specific reason for sailing into Port Vathy: we had read that it housed a small colony of potters, and we had run our own studio pottery in England for many years so naturally were eager to see what was going on in other countries.

So we rowed ashore, taking with us swimming costumes so that we could enjoy bathing off the brilliant white sands. Our original idea was to buy some food at the local shop and have a picnic lunch on the beach, but there was a setback – there didn't appear to be a shop in this very small community. Fortunately we managed to persuade the owner of the taverna to sell us some fresh bread and goat's cheese, and a large melon.

While engaged in this transaction we realised that we had practically no food on the boat for our evening meal and if there was no shop, well ... the obvious solution would be to eat out at the taverna, and it would make a pleasant change, too. The owner was quite agreeable, merely asking that we should give him our orders there and then so that he could be sure to have the food ready. So we ordered our mixture of steaks and local red mullet and green beans and chips, even an omelette for the vegetarian among us, and arranged to come over about eight o'clock. Then off we went on our mid-day swim.

While walking along the edge of the beach we kept our eyes open for potteries, and made a strange discovery. Though we spied four or five houses with large pottery kilns adjoining, they were all empty, just shells of some previous existence. It was almost as if the occupants had just suddenly got up and gone leaving everything as it was – indeed, the kilns were still half full of fired pots. We began to fear our quest was in vain, and then, rather thankfully, during the lunch time siesta spied a man in clay-stained overalls walking along the beach from a cluster of buildings in the far corner, obviously homeward bound for his mid-day siesta. There at least, obviously, was one working pottery.

After our bathe and lunch, washed down with some cool Samos wine, we climbed round to the far side and there sure enough found a peasant pottery working at high pressure –

and how simply organised! First clay was dug out of the side of the surrounding hills, then loaded on to baskets tied to donkeys, and then brought down to large cleaning pools. There were three large brick kilns with huge fire places underneath, and these were, with equal simplicity and economy, fired with brushwood which again was brought down on the donkeys from the hillside. We were most impressed, and liked the simple peasant ware, buying several pieces as presents; and we enjoyed talking, mostly in sign language, with the two old potters and their sons.

Altogether it was a most rewarding afternoon and we felt pretty pleased with life when at last we walked back to our old inflatable and rowed back to *Sanu* (which all day had nestled luxuriously at anchor in the middle of a glassy sheet of calm water). Once aboard *Sanu* we set about cleaning and tidying ourselves in preparation for our gaily anticipated outing that evening.

It was then, as the story teller might say with a meaningful look, that our luck ran out. One moment we were lying peacefully at anchor, the next the sea around us was a mass of turbulence, the boat rocked violently and we were enveloped by huge gusts of winds hurtling down from the mountains. What had been described as a completely sheltered anchorage was now not far removed from being in the open sea, and our bow reared and plunged, jerking awkwardly on the anchor chain.

It was about seven o'clock when the wind began to blow. Within a short time it dawned on us that we were going to have a problem getting ashore. Unfortunately our Seagull outboard engine was out of action which meant we would have to row. We didn't like the look of the waves swishing past – still we were prepared to have a go. Alan got into the inflatable, fixed the oars and was cast off to see how he might manage (with us keeping a long rope attached for safety). Alas, within seconds Alan had been whirled round and carried seawards, and it took us all our time to manage to drag him back by the skin of his inflatable.

'Well,' I said rather miserably. 'It's no go then.'

By now dusk had fallen and the bright outside lights of the taverna had been switched on, no doubt ready to give the foreign visitors a royal welcome. Worse still, we could even smell the scent of luscious cooking, for we weren't very far away as the crow flies. Alas, we might as well have been a hundred miles awy! Eight o'clock came and went, half past, and then nine o'clock. All around the waves were hissing and spraying and slapping against the sides of the boat, some of them quite mountainous for a 'protected' bay ... there could simply be no question of trying to row ashore in such conditions.

What made everything so maddening, apart from the tantalising aromas being wafted in our direction, was the knowledge that our own supplies were literally down to bread and soup – precisely what we finally sat down to in *Sanu*'s long saloon at about ten o'clock. It was a sober, sad meal. Before going to bed we had a conference about safety. We had our very stout old fisherman anchor out, with over a hundred feet of chain, in a depth of sixteen feet – surely that would hold? Well, just to be on the safe side Jess and I would keep an eye on things from the vantage point of our deck cabin.

For the next two or three hours I kept padding around the deck checking on our position, then snuggling back into bed for a fitful doze. I was too worried to really drop off, but must have temporarily relaxed – only to be jerked into wakefulness by an alarming sort of general pandemonium. My ears resounded to the raucous noise of horns blowing – what on earth? Why, it was someone blaring on a foghorn ... A moment later there was a tremendous flash and the whole night sky was brilliantly floodlit. Good Heavens, a flare – someone was firing a flare, they must be in trouble, sinking or something.

Without stopping even to put on my trousers, I raced on to the brilliantly illuminated deck and stood there, dazed and naked, staring around. Everywhere the waters were seething and frothing – and there, over to my left, was the source of the light and sound, a small yacht flying the Swiss flag which was our only companion at the anchorage.

'It's that yacht – he must be in trouble!' I shouted. 'Come quickly, let's see what we can do –'

I was about to issue some positive instructions to the others as they came rushing on deck when a sudden suspicion began niggling at me. A moment later it was confirmed by Stephen.

'Dad! Hey, we're *dragging*!'

A quick look confirmed the alarming truth, and at once the penny clicked. Our Swiss neighbour was not in dire trouble – *we were*. By good fortune he had been awake and noticed *Sanu* had begun to move her position, and indeed now was moving quite rapidly.

'Quick, throw out the second anchor,' I shouted to Alan. 'Come on, Stephen, we'll start the engine.'

Alan threw out our Danforth on a hundred foot length of rope – maybe it couldn't achieve much but it might slow down progress to give us some breathing space. Meantime Stephen and I raced down into the engine room, switched on the lights, prayed that our recently troublesome magneto would not play us up – and embarked on the petrifyingly slow process of hand-turning an old Kelvin 88 hp diesel which anyway has to start on petrol and then switch over to diesel. Sometimes this can take as long as half an hour, though in all fairness nine times out of ten the engine catches on the first turn.

Thank goodness this was one of those occasions: relieved I ran up to the wheelhouse to take charge of the controls while Stephen joined the others in the laborious task of winching in two anchors, both out more than a hundred feet. While they did this I peered about me in the darkness, trying to familiarise myself with the shadowy outline of nearby cliffs. What a good thing we had spent the day ashore and I was roughly familiar with the semi-circular shape of the bay.

At last the anchors were up and cautiously I put *Sanu* into gear and took us in a wide sweep around the middle, deeper part of the bay, using the anchor-light of the Swiss yacht as a guide line. It took a good twenty minutes or so for our manoeuvring, but at last we managed to line *Sanu* up in much the same position as before, and this time we were careful to drop both our anchors.

'Thank you!' I called out to the Swiss yacht, before we finally returned to bed again. 'Thanks very much!'

Back in bed I knew it would be impossible to sleep, so left the cabin door open and lay there meditating. Supposing ...? I was still lost in my uneasy thoughts when, unbelievably, the horn began blaring out again. Rushing out on to deck I saw that we were fractionally a little nearer to the Swiss yacht. We must have dragged just a little, but maybe we would have held at that – but unfortunately our neighbour was quite understandably worried.

'Can you *please* to let me know if you are going to *move* your boat further away?'

I swore to myself, but felt we owed it to him to move. However I could not face going through all the weary process of re-anchoring. I looked at the clock, it was nearly half past three. We had been due in any case to set off at dawn on a forty mile crossing to Hydra, near the Greek mainland. We might just as well start now.

'Come along, Stephen – we're off to Hydra.'

I spoke too soon. Sure enough we started the engine and upped our anchors and headed out of the bay. We knew that the weather outside was hardly likely to be exactly calm, but were relieved for the first few miles to enjoy a lee protection from Siphnos. Then, when at last we left that shelter – all at once the waves came rolling down on our beam and life became very uncomfortable. Still we have become used to *Sanu*'s ability to cope with such conditions, and we decided to press on for Hydra.

I handed the wheel over to Alan and went into my cabin to try and rest – but of course it was impossible, with all the heaving. At last after an extra large movement, the sort to bring the proverbial heart into one's mouth, I dressed and went back to the wheelhouse. Alan was struggling ferociously with the wheel, obviously in some difficulties. In the semi-darkness I could sense his perturbance: looking ahead at the great white crested waves I soon began to share it.

'What's that light over there?' said Alan, rather meaningly, pointing to a winking light on our starboard.

'That's a lighthouse off the South of Seriphos, the next island up.'

I know what Alan had in mind and was rapidly finding myself in total agreement. Another huge wave hit our side and made up my mind.

'You're right, of course, bring her round and head for the lighthouse will you, Alan?'

The next two hours were by no means comfortable, but nothing like as bad as taking the waves sideways. Now our high bow headed straight into them we hardly rocked at all as, by the light of a bleak dawn, we drew nearer to what looked, and indeed was to prove, a barren and inhospitable sort of island.

Seriphos was that, indeed. Despite what had just happened to us at Siphnos I felt curiously drawn to that island, and have often thought if I had to chose a Greek island for a home that would be it – even that self-same bay! But for Seriphos I can not find a single good word to say. I was not surprised to read somewhere that the island had always been renowned for its poverty, and there was actually a Greek phrase to describe an old maid – 'an old woman of Seriphos'. It was just that sort of place – barren, brown, bovine and bleak.

We sensed that our troubles were not over, even from the moment we anchored well up in Livardhi Bay and found ourselves still subject to gusty winds blowing in from the mountains. So strong were the winds that in the end, observing the practice of two or three other yachts anchored about is, we decided to take a very long rope forward and tie the end round one of the stout trees lining the shore – thus giving added anchorage.

Even then we felt uneasy. Suppose the rope gave way, and we depended entirely on our anchor? Was that anchor going to hold? We had some discussions, and Stephen came up with a bright idea.

'Under water the anchor won't weigh much ... What say I put on my snorkel and go and move it further into the shore?'

Incredible as the idea may sound, this is precisely what Stephen did. We all leaned over the bow of the boat and watched: it really was a weird sight to see this slender figure in bathing trunks bending down and dragging a 160 lb anchor fifty feet or so along the bed of the ocean before dropping it firmly into the sands!

So far, I suppose so good. At least we did not drag or come to any great harm. But we were not happy at all. We were by now overdue at Hydra, where we had arranged to meet Genny's friend, Sheldon.

Already he must be standing on the quayside anxiously scanning the horizon for some sign of his saviours. Time to be off.

The next morning we were up at 6 a.m., for it was a forty mile trip and I wanted to make sure we reached Hydra before the bewitching afternoon hour when all berths in the harbour were taken by other yachts. The engine started and off we went down the long neck of Livardhi Bay. Outside the sea seemed rather rough but we were still protected by being in the lee of the island. On we went, three and four miles, and then suddenly – wham, we had lost our protection, and huge white waves came bearing down upon us (on our · *side,* of course, *Sanu* specialises in always having to travel *across* rough seas). We rolled and rolled, the bell rang several times; we were in for a rough voyage.

All the same, we were all grimly determined to get to Hydra by hook or crook ... until it suddenly became sadly apparent that crook would stop us.

Stephen came into the wheelhouse with a grave look.

'Hey, I've just been down in the engine room ... it's started to move again. Only very slightly but – well, you remember it happened once before.'

I did remember indeed: how could I ever forget? About three years ago we had been caught in a cyclone crossing the Gulf of Lions, off the coast of Southern France – at the height of all the rough seas Stephen had been terrified to see the huge Kelvin engine moving slightly on its foundations. Being a young man of courage and enterprise he had hurriedly gathered together half a dozen strong wooden wedges which we always keep on hand and somehow managed to hammer them in such a way as to stop the engine's movements. When we finally got into port we found that the foundation bolts had worked loose ... no doubt this had happened again, as a result of our recent rough weather.

'Well,' I said resignedly. 'We simply can't risk going forty miles in a sea like this with a moving engine.'

'I'll say not,' said Stephen. 'But don't worry – I can soon fix it once we get into some shelter.'

'Getting into some shelter' was to prove a laughable phrase. Because we had travelled some seven miles up the side of Seriphos, away from Livardhi, I decided not to go all the way back there, but to head instead for a nearer bay mentioned in Captain Denham's book, Koutala – 'which is spacious and similar to Livardhi, and has two mooring buoys and iron ore tips.'

Soon we could see the bay opening out. It seemed to be well sheltered by the mountains – but why then were there white-cap waves everywhere? Why indeed – the fact was this was one of those accursed spots where sea conditions were catastrophically affected by mountain winds, gusts of which came hurtling down creating quite rough seas even in a sheltered spot.

Well, there could be no going back now. We would just have to find one of those buoys that Captain Denham mentioned and tie up to it. At least we could then feel secure.

I brought *Sanu* closer to the shore and we began looking around. Yes, there along the hills were signs of iron ore tips and workings – though they did look curiously derelict. Oh, and there was the pier where the iron ore steamers must have loaded. But surely, why, the pier was all broken up – it couldn't be in use any longer.

What then of the two buoys? At first we couldn't see either, and one we never saw, but quite later on we spied the faint rusty colour of a single buoy, placed rather too close to the rocky cliffs for our liking. Still it was obviously one of the buoys which the cargo boats would have used while waiting their turn: it was certain to be very heavy, and should be safe enough for *Sanu*. With considerable difficulty I manoeuvred the heaving boat close to the buoy until Stephen was able to take a running jump, clutching a rope in his hand. While he tied up I reversed madly to save us being carried beyond. Meantime Alan and the others threw Stephen another rope, and then a chain, so that we ended up being bounded to the buoy by three separate lifelines.

'At least we're not likely to break away from the buoy,' I said with some satisfaction.

My satisfaction was short lived: it lasted only until Stephen and I rowed ashore to the nearby sandy beach – and came across the very old, very rusty iron chain which led from a bollard high up on the beach, down into the water. At the other end was tied the buoy to which *Sanu* clung. Quite obviously the buoy had not been used for a long time, for the iron ore works must have been closed for some years ... this meant that the buoy probably hadn't been checked for years, either.

'My God, Stephen,' I stared back to where *Sanu*'s bow kept rising violently into the waves' motion, tugging each time at the buoy. 'Do you think the buoy will hold?'

'I don't know, Dad.' Stephen looked worried: that alarmed me, as Stephen seldom looks worried. 'I just don't know.' He shrugged. 'Let's hope so.' He looked thoughtful. 'I think we'd better keep an anchor watch tonight – just in case.'

In the end the weather deteriorated so badly that we did better than have an anchor watch: Stephen and I went down into the engine room about midnight and started up our engine. We both knew that if the buoy should give way there would be no time at all for us to run down and start the engine – we would be on the rocks in less than a minute. Now, however, with the engine humming away, we really could relax a bit – in less than a minute we could put *Sanu* into gear and steam away from danger should it prove necessary.

I am glad to say that it did not, and in fact perhaps I have maligned those good people of Seriphos who may be responsible for the condition of that buoy. At all events both buoy and chain, and of course our own ropes and chain, all held well and truly for the three days we were to spend in that exposed and uncomfortable anchorage.

Three days ... and we only had food for one day aboard! Once again we were caught out, as we had been at Siphnos. This time things were more serious, for when we went ashore expecting to find at least a small shop, we found an area of desolation. Lining the long beach were simply half a dozen cottages, all of them tumbledown and inhabited by very poor-looking families, probably left over from the days when the iron ore works were in being.

In desperation, when it became obvious there was no other way of obtaining food, I began knocking at doors to inquire if I may buy some bread and cheese, perhaps some fruit? As always in Greece the people were strangely dignified, despite their obvious poverty, and though they could not speak English, nor I Greek, they seemed to understand something of our requirements. One dear old lady went away and came back bearing a huge bunch of grapes which she thrust into my hands – but no question of payment, she just wouldn't accept a penny.

Very much embarrassed I felt like throwing in the sponge, but I knew there wasn't a scrap of bread on the boat so kept on knocking until, at one house, after the woman had at first refused, her husband came up and said something to her and she went away and produced one large loaf for which I was allowed to pay 10 drachmas. Bearing this somewhat inadequate offering, plus the grapes, we rowed back to *Sanu* for a very frugal supper.

The next morning, when it was obvious that the weather was still too rough for us to think of going to Hydra, Alan announced a drastic decision.

'Look, we simply must have some food. I'm ready to walk over the mountains to the nearest town. Anyone else want to come?'

First I looked at our chart and found that the nearest town was in fact Livardhi, where we had originally moored.

'It's eight miles away,' I said.

'Never mind,' said Alan. 'Do my figure good.'

In the end Stephen and Gina decided to accompany Alan,

and off they went, about nine o'clock, each carrying a rucksack or bag. I watched them through binoculars until the three tiny specks had disappeared over the top of the first mountain.

After that it was a question of settling down and waiting. Two o'clock, three o'clock four o'clock ... Just as we were beginning to get worried, I spied a solitary figure through the binoculars – Alan, bowed down under a huge rucksack. A little later there was Stephen, and still further behind Gina. They all looked pretty weary – not surprising, as they had walked a total of sixteen miles.

Their final arrival, fortunately, was a triumphal one. They came bearing better than alms – food, and lots of food, including what they declared was the only chicken on the whole island. Jess gave three cheers and sped off down to the galley to start preparing a Gargantuan feast.

Meantime the wind was howling worse than ever, the waves slapped against the sides of the boat, and we were thoroughly glad we were tied up to this proven reliable buoy and not out in the open sea.

Others were, however! About an hour later, not long before our meal was due, we heard much shouting and banging outside: we rushed onto deck and found a tiny Greek caique attempting to tie up to the buoy. With the rough conditions they were having great difficulty, so we indicated they should tie up to our stern. A little while later, with a helping hand, the three crew members – the men and a young boy – clambered upon *Sanu*.

'Eight!' one of the men kept saying at the top of his voice, rolling his eyes, 'Eight! Eight!'

We decided he meant Force Eight – 'out there' – and guessed this to be, if anything, an understatement. The men and the boy looked thoroughly worn out, and we felt the least we could do was ask them down into the saloon for a warm drink of brandy. After that, despite the language problem, relations became so cordial that we prevailed on them to stay for the meal. It was, indeed, a case of dividing the bread between more mouths – but as so often is the case in such circumstances the reward was a real one in terms of human contact. Before the evening was over the men were opening wallets and showing us pictures of their families, and we were showing off our pictures, too.

Although communication was difficult the older man, the skipper, spoke a little Italian and French and managed to elucidate some sort of picture of their background. They lived on Kalimnos, a small Greek island off the coast of Turkey, and earned their living sponge diving. They often made quite long trips – we were amazed to see the frailty of their boat, which only has half covered cabin and half open wheelhouse – in this they had travelled a hundred miles in rough open seas! Apparently they earned quite a reasonable living, though it was obvious from the figures they quoted for what they were paid for sponge – compared to the price we had noticed being charged in Mykonos and Hydra – that as usual, the middle-men, were making the real profit.

Before they went back to their boat to sleep the men rather shyly produced some sponges and presented them to us. In the morning, silently, they had gone.

It was time for us to be off, too. We could not be sure how much the weather had improved, but certainly in the bay the wind had died down, and we hoped that out at sea the improvement might be maintained. Alas, we were wrong – once we had left the lee of the island the waves were almost as rough as when we had set out three days previously. But this time the engine was secure and we were all so sick of Seriphos that I think it would have taken a full scale gale to have stopped us setting out for Hydra.

It was not a comfortable trip, but we made it safely enough, and came gliding into the shelter of Hydra harbour at about four o'clock on a Saturday afternoon. We had originally been due on the Monday and we were afraid that Sheldon would have got fed up with waiting and gone on to Piraeus, our next destination. At first our fears seemed proven when an American yachtsman strolled over and said, 'Ah, *here* you are *Sanu* – a fellow's been looking for you for days. Afraid he must have given you up.'

Fortunately, soon after that as we were relaxing in the lovely sunshine, far removed from meltemi madness – who should come bounding up the gangway but Sheldon, his eyes blinking excitedly behind his large horn-rimmed glasses.

'Hey there!' he said cheerfully. 'What luck. I was going to catch the evening ferry back to Piraeus. Well, now – have you had a good trip?'

It took us most of the rest of our two days stay at Hydra to tell Sheldon all about our trip – in particular the last few days of it. Somehow I don't think he fully appreciated all that we had been through, for at the end of it, all he said really was, 'Great – say, I'm really looking forward to my first trip with you to Piraeus.'

XII
The Athens Bus

For sheer 18 carat melodrama, a trauma every hour you might almost say, the very last leg of our Greek cruise took some beating. Perhaps the impact was made more vivid by the fact that until the past few days the whole of our cruise had been carried out quite peacefully, a dreamy period bereft of any of the usual nautical problems. Courses had proved accurate, landfalls made as planned, there had been no going aground, no unexpected accidents, all systems had worked perfectly, except for the comparatively minor problem of our magneto. Why, I had even begun to think upon it as our most trouble-free cruise.

And then came the forty mile trip back to Piraeus, where we had decided to leave *Sanu* for the winter. Actually behind this decision lay quite formidable internal wranglings. In the first place I had always intended that our trip should end up back in Malta, where the berthing was safe and comparatively cheap, as we knew from experience. Unfortunately during the course of our cruise, what with the oil crisis and the Greek-Turkey war, economic conditions had changed so much that the cost of fuel alone had gone up astronomically. Getting *Sanu* back to Malta would have cost a great deal more than originally anticipated – added to which the diciness of our magneto, which we knew had only been patched up, not cured, made the risk of a five hundred mile journey across the open sea seem too great.

Thinking on these lines – together with the appreciation

that in the following year we would very likely want to continue wandering about Greece – had persuaded us that it might be better to find a home for *Sanu* in Greek waters. This was where the arguments came in. Although she had never been there Jess had become convinced that Spetsai, where Charles Rayner wintered his boat, would be a good spot in which to leave *Sanu*. I, on the other hand, felt more drawn to Zea Marina, Piraeus, which we had seen and knew to be extremely safe and sheltered (whereas in fact I remembered Charles had confessed to me that our draught of $7\frac{1}{2}$ feet might create problems at Spetsai, where the depth in the harbour was about 10 foot but dropping by $2\frac{1}{2}$ feet in the winter. The more Jess argued one way, the more stubbornly I planned the other. In the end it was agreed we should go to Piraeus – but even as the apparent victory was won I had an uneasy suspicion that, as so often has proved the case, Jess might well prove to have been right (she has!)

So off to Piraeus we went, one glorious sunny September morning, the sea around Hydra a comfortable calm and everything auguring for a delightful six hour cruise ... all of which gave the utmost pleasure to our new recruit. Sheldon, who kept pacing about the boat, or standing up in the bow shading his eyes, and searching the passing countryside of Hydra, to our right, the mainland to our left.

'Gosh, it's great, Denys! I *am* enjoying this ... Do you think I could have a go at steering some time?'

'By all means, Sheldon. I'll show you how. You stand here and hold the wheel like that, and keep your eye on the compass ... The course is actually 30°, but you don't have to be too exact – as long as you keep the indicator between 20° and 30°, that will be OK.'

Somewhat apprehensively I left Sheldon at the wheel and went and stood on the bow, looking back at our wake. As I feared within a short time *Sanu* began to veer off dramatically to one side. I went back to the wheelhouse and corrected the steering, then told Sheldon to hold the wheel carefully in place but to be sure to compensate for any variations. He was very willing, but obviously found things rather difficult, as most people do when they first take over the steering of any boat.

In the middle of all this Gill brought up some appetising dishes of salad and cheese and fruit, and we enjoyed our last lunch at sea on *Sanu*, somewhere off the island of Poros, and heading for Aegina, looming on the horizon. We were well on our way, almost half way in fact – but what was this? The boat was beginning to rock, there could be no doubt. Looking around I could see that the calm had gone and there was a general choppiness, though nothing really to worry about.

Just to be on the safe side Gill took over the wheel from Sheldon, and we steered on, coming up to the coastline of Aegina. Soon it would be time to be looking ahead through the slight heat haze, hoping to see the distant rooftops of Piraeus. Yes, it was really all going very nicely, despite the slight choppiness.

Suddenly, in a stroke, the whole peaceful picture was changed. It was an experience not altogether unfamiliar to regular *Sanu* travellers – a happening that usually occurred at least once a summer cruise. One moment *Sanu* was ploughing valiantly through the sea, sending a long creamy wake behind her, the old Kelvin engine roaring steadily away – the next moment there was simply a great silence, the bow of the ship began to waver as she lost way, and the wake faded into nothingness ...

I came up from the stern of the boat, where I had been standing lost in thought, just in time to see Stephen disappearing down into the engine room. Miserably, my heart suddenly down in my boots, I followed him down. Everything was hot and steamy and oily – and wrapped in mysterious silence.

'What do you think's the matter, Stephen?'

'How the hell should I know?'

'Well, you're the engineer ...'

Stephen and I fell immediately into our inevitable cross talk which covers up our apprehension when things go wrong. The wronger they become the more violent our conversations: other people aboard *Sanu*, we were amused to learn, are terrified to come near the engine room at such times ... in fact, we were merely following out a protective ritual, whose actual words meant very little.

'Probably dirty fuel,' Stephen decided after a while, and set about the laborious task of unscrewing our two diesel filters and cleaning them out – all this while *Sanu* rolled from side to side.

All this took time, perhaps twenty minutes or so ... twenty minutes in which the all pervading dominating single factor was the complete silence, the dreadful absence of that familiar humming sound of the Kelvin engine pounding away.

At last Stephen had finished, the pieces were reconnected, and we began the laborious task of trying to start the engine again. Always at such times, when it is very hot, the engine is the very devil to start, and this time was no exception. Indeed, not only was it no exception – it proved to be a non-starter. Nothing we could do, either separately or together, could coax the old Kelvin back into life.

Time was passing. And anyway, what was happening to *Sanu*? Wouldn't we be drifting dangerously? Worried, I ran up on to deck and scanned the horizon, half afraid I might see jagged rocks in the offing – in which case heaven knows what we could have done, save for throwing over an anchor if the water was shallow enough. Fortunately the land still seemed a good distance away: the island of Aegina to our port, and Piraeus and the mainland somewhere to starboard.

While I was momentarily on deck I caught a glimpse of Sheldon standing uncertainly in the bow. He looked at me inquiringly.

'Some little problem, eh?'

'Yes,' I nodded reassuringly. 'Not to worry.'

Then I went back to the engine room and plunged back into my world of very real worry. By now Stephen had given up the main engine and was concentrating on trying to start the second engine, our Lister which we had had put in solely for such emergencies. Unfortunately, despite the fact that earlier in the trip we had run it on one or two occasions, now it too would not start, probably for the same reason, blocked fuel pipes. We began to have an uneasy suspicion that someone had sold us dirty fuel, probably at Naxos.

Time continued to pass. One hour and then two. It was after four o'clock, soon coming towards five. Now a new problem haunted me. Before very long it would be getting dark. I didn't want us to be stuck out here in the dark with no engines ...

'Come on Stephen – we simply *must* get the main engine going. Leave the little one – it's the Kelvin or –'

I didn't finish the sentence and we went back to trying to start the Kelvin. After another half hour of that Stephen finished my sentence for me.

'Dad, this isn't going to work. We're indeed in trouble. I'm telling you.'

Unlike me Stephen is very slow to panic, but when he does it comes over in a big way and he becomes convinced that everything is beyond hope. Usually, paradoxically, at such moments things began to work. This was no exception. I gave the last desperate swing on the engine and there was an unexpected clattering as the cylinders began to fire on petrol.

'Injectors!' I screamed at Stephen. Like a madman he whirled shut the four injector taps, while I clamped over the big change over lever. There was an awesome pause – and then suddenly the familiar deep throated roar of the Kelvin starting to work on diesel. We were in business again!

Stephen, however, was not to be lightly appeased. He shook his head worriedly.

'Don't like the sound of the engine. It's not right. There must be something wrong.'

I listened, apprehensively. There was nothing wrong. It was a good healthy note. I looked at Stephen and realised he was still caught up in a sort of disaster syndrome, almost willing something to be going wrong. I took him by the arm and shook him reassuringly.

'Don't be silly. There's nothing wrong. It's your imagination. Come on, let's get going.'

Fortunately I was right. The engine ran perfectly. Soon we were steaming towards Piraeus. On deck everyone relaxed almost excessively. There was a babble of cheerful conversations, and we all began confessing what had been our secret dreads during our three hours of drifting. Surprisingly enough, that drift had been quite minimal; we could not have covered more than a mile or so, gently on a collision course with still distant Aegina.

Now I went up into the bow and began searching for the landmarks of Piraeus. I was glad we had been there before, so that the approach was not a strange one. I looked at the clock in the wheelhouse. We still had a couple of hours before dusk, and we could not be more than an hour away.

Soon, sure enough, we saw the outline of Piraeus, and the little island marking the entrance to Zea Marina. It was still quite empty, but this no longer bothered us ... soon we would be within the shelter of the harbour walls, tying up at a berth.

It was a heartening thought ... but Fate had not finished with us that traumatic day. Whenever our engine stops while running in gear one of the after effects is that the gears are jammed and have to be freed. We had carried out this operation but naturally had not had an opportunity yet to check that the change back from forward to neutral was working properly again. Just as we came round the bend into the main harbour entrance I became obsessed with the worrying thought – supposing the gears were jammed again – we would drive straight into all those parked yachts and cause havoc. Better, I decided, to try out the gear change now, before we got into too confined a space.

I throttled down, and turned the gear handle to put the engine into neutral.

Nothing happened, the handle went round and round ... and round. The gears were not working!

'Stephen – the gears!'

Like a flash Stephen was down into the engine room, coming up a moment later with a look of anguish.

'The gear chain's broken – one of the links has snapped.'

Desperately I looked around. We were heading towards a sort of parking buoy moored in the middle of the main entrance for the convenience of boats when they first arrived. Could we possibly get a rope on to that?

'Alan – quick – Take a rope – you'll have to dive in and swim to the buoy and try and tie it on.'

Poor Alan, who a few minutes before had been sun-bathing in utter oblivion, suddenly, rather dazedly, found himself in his bathing trunks poised on the edge of the boat, diving into the murky waters.

Brave Alan, too, for he managed to get to the buoy and somehow to clamber on it, cutting himself on the rough barnacled underside of the buoy. Bleeding profusely, he tried to tie the rope on – but of course, still in gear, *Sanu* glided right past the buoy and the rope was whipped away out of Alan's grasp.

Desperately I looked about me. At least we had room to manoeuvre. There was poor Alan stranded on the buoy that was rapidly receding behind us – but at least there was room for me to bring *Sanu* round in a wide circle and come up again to the buoy. But if we remained in gear, how were we going to get tied up? We simply had to stop the boat somehow.

'The engine,' said Stephen quickly. 'We'll just have to stop the engine next time we come up to the buoy ... then get a rope on before it's too late. Quick, someone stand at the top of the engine room and I'll go down – give a shout when you want the engine shut off.'

It was a terrifying prospect of shut stop timing – but our only chance. I shut the throttle down to the very minimum and headed *Sanu* towards the buoy. The others had tied together five lengths of rope and were all ready to heave the end over to Alan, on the buoy. Slowly we came up ... at the crucial moment I shouted out for Stephen to shut off the engine. We glided steadily up to the buoy, unable of course, in any way to hasten our gradual slowing up ... Over went the rope, Alan grabbed it, like a demon would it round the hook on the buoy ... We drifted on, but more slowly, the rope took the straining – and held. Moments later *Sanu* had come to rest, securely tied up to the buoy.

Typically of officialdom, within seconds a fast motor boat from the Marina office had come out to tell us with wild gestures that we could not stay tied to the buoy, a large ship was coming in any moment. Fortunately it did not take us more than ten minutes to repair the gear chain – equally fortunately this time the engine started quite quickly. After rescuing a bloody and indeed shattered Alan, we resumed the short remainder of our voyage into the heart of the Marina.

Even then we had another traumatic experience. We found there was not a single berth left for us to work our way into – not an inch to spare! In the end, in desperation, we somehow anchored among some small dinghies, keeping *Sanu* twenty feet out from the shallow embankment – impossible as a permanent berth, adequate for a night's rest. Then we all flopped down completely shattered.

The next morning, overwhelmed by a depressed certainty that we would never find a berth and would have to leave Zea Marina and seek shelter somewhere else, I was sitting morosely on the bow and looking across the Marina when to my utter astonishment I saw the crew of a big yacht actually winding in their anchor, preparatory to sailing away.

'A berth! A berth!'

In seconds Stephen and I were down starting the engine. The yacht had hardly left its berth before we were heading *Sanu* over. Just as well, too, for we had only just tied up in what looked like one of the best and safest berths in the whole Marina when another yacht came sailing up, looking hopefully for a berth.

Not surprisingly, the reaction to our last trip of the summer cruise was – well, a real reaction. Both Stephen and I felt as if we never wanted to go to sea again; we had had enough of *Sanu* and all her trials and tribulations, we couldn't wait to get back to dry land – indeed to good old Cornwall, far from all this meltemi nonsense. The others felt much the same, I fancy, though in a way they were always a little less emotionally involved than Stephen and I. For both of us *Sanu* has become a kind of many headed monster, that we love and hate, which binds our lives. For myself, I do not really complain, deep down, because of all the magic the boat has provided – but on Stephen's behalf I feel rather guilty, fearing that our perpetual dependency on him as engineer must condition his life.

For the moment, at any rate, Stephen's life, like our own, was able to settle down to a gloriously peaceful relaxation in the safety of Zea Marina. The boat was snugly tied up, with two anchors out, and four ropes binding her to the quay. We had all the water we wanted, plenty of shops within a few minutes walk. A little van came round with ice and cold drinks ... all around us were lots of interesting boats preparing to hibernate for the winter. What more could we ask? Just relax ...

For nearly a week we did exactly that: then, rather sadly the party began to break up. The first to go were Gill and Alan, those staunch and regular devotees of *Sanu* cruises. Like Demelza and Diana before them they had managed to fly out to Athens on a cheap return, and now the time limit had nearly expired. After one last shopping spree in Athens, ferreting around the market of the Plakka, late one evening we waved them goodbye as they set off for their air port, poor Alan almost completely hidden by a huge back-pack.

Genny and Sheldon were to be the next to go – only theirs was to be no ordinary journey. Piraeus, in fact, was to mark the final parting of the ways between Genevieve and her rather sad parents. Faced with the choice of going back to art school in Redruth or accompanying Sheldon on a long trip to India and Nepal, possibly after that Japan and South America, Genevieve – wisely we had to agree – you only live once! – had chosen the bigger and wider adventure. At the end of the week she and Sheldon would be flying out to New Delhi, preparatory to a trip up into the Himalayas, where Sheldon hoped to do some filming.

Before they left, however, we had the pleasure of seeing our first sample of Sheldon's work as a film director. Apparently he was quite well known among underground film makers, and had regularly produced and directed a dozen films. His last and most adventurous production had been a 50-minute film about a group of Tibetan monks who had left their seclusion up in the Himalayan mountains and made a trip to London and Europe giving public performances of their religious ceremonies (which included a lot of complicated chantings).

Sheldon had brought a copy of this film with him and was determined that Jess and I should be treated to a private showing, and we thought it showed great enterprise on his behalf actually to arrange a showing at the Goethe Institute Athens. It was a little strange attending a cinema show where the seven of us were the only audience, but as soon as the brilliant colours of the Tibetan monks and their costumes and ways of life appeared on the screen we soon found ourselves engrossed.

We were most intrigued by the filming of life over in the Himalayas – also by some remarkable old film of life in Tibet itself before the Chinese take-over – and we appreciated the skill with which Sheldon had woven in the later episodes of the monks arriving by coach in London.

Most of the film was given up to an actual live concert in a big church in France, and perhaps here there was rather a surfeit of deep chants and rolling eyes – but it was all very expertly done. We felt relieved to know that Sheldon was certainly no layabout, like so many of his country men we had seen on the trip, but a professional and dedicated film-maker.

But alas, this dedicated professional was about to take away our little 'baby'. So, I suppose, our sentimental old minds used to ponder ... though to be honest, once or twice I would snatch a look at the extremely well developed and rather beautiful 'baby' and think – well who could really blame Sheldon. Lucky man!

Amusingly, before they left, Sheldon had a taste of an unfamiliar and rather disagreeable side of my nature, which fortunately I manage to keep generally under control. One day there had been a lot of rather large talk about Sheldon cooking us a great meal – in the end, through no fault of his own (as it happened as he was busily rushing around trying to finish fixing up the film), Sheldon left it too late to buy in any food, so that we had to have a rather mediocre scratch meal of pizzas brought from a shop. By the time these finally arrived I was glowering and sulky, and said lots of nasty and petty things to Sheldon, rather as if he was one of my children. Looking back I feel he took it all very amiably – perhaps really he liked being made to feel one of the family. At any rate I had to admit he earned my grudging respect, for the next day he went out of his way to make us a really grand meal, and a vegetarian one at that!

The day after was a very sad one for Jess and I. Suddenly Genevieve was leaving. All day she and Sheldon accumulated their variegated bags, piling them high upon the sundrenched deck. At eleven o'clock at night with Stephen's aid we carried all the bags along the quay to the nearest road, there standing in desultory conversation until the ever resourceful Sheldon appeared in a taxi. A quick kiss and cuddle, a few last endearments – and we were waving to a tiny round face peering out of the back of the taxi. Moments later Genny and Sheldon were swept out of our view, en route for a destination 8000 miles away ...

Suddenly, from a one-time complement of thirteen gay people *Sanu*'s register had dwindled to a rather lonely four, Gina and Stephen, Jess and myself. We all felt rather desolate, but fortunately there was a great deal to do. First I had to make arrangements not only for the boat to stay in the berth for the winter, but also for someone to keep an eye on her moorings, pump out the bilges, etc.

Here we seemed to be in luck's way; we had made the acquaintance of a young American, Peter Schmidt, who lived on a small yacht nearby who would be spending the winter at Zea Marina. He already looked after two or three other boats and would be glad to do the same for *Sanu*. We agreed terms and had Peter and his wife over for an interesting meal, when Mrs Schmidt gave us a vivid account of her recent experience as cook on one of the big charter boats. It had been just like a luxury hotel, she said – the whole of the food for a two week trip, except for a few fresh items like bread and fruit, had been loaded up into a deep freeze before ever setting off, and there was every kind of gadget to make her job easier. It all sounded very pleasant, money for jam so to speak – until she mentioned rather wearily, 'the meltemi' – We knew exactly how she felt!

Now Stephen and I busied ourselves with tidying up the engine room, checking equipment, and so on, while Jess and

Gina did some spring cleaning down in the saloon. We always tried to leave *Sanu* tidy and neat, though we were uneasily aware, as ever, that we had not really solved the problem of deck leaks. At least we would cut out after deck leaks by spreading our orange canopy right across the stern portion.

The last few days went quickly: there were endless washing of clothes, of sheets, of blankets – then the stove taken to pieces – finally all the crockery and pots and pans to be cleaned. It was all exhausting work ... and on top of all this Jess and I had to keep on egging Gina and Stephen to go into Athens and sell a ring of Gina's. Money for the return trip was very low, and we had to all pool our resources in every way.

Miserably the day of departure drew nearer. On our last evening in Piraeus we had a final meal at the American Pizza House, where the biggest pizzas in the world, we felt sure, are served ... and then popped into one of the rooftop open air cinemas, to see an English film, *O Lucky Man*. Well, we had been lucky, too, that summer – we had three marvellous months of the Greek Isles syndrome – we could not really complain.

Then back to *Sanu* for a last night uneasy sleep, among all the piled baggages – ready to be off at five in the morning.

I can't quite remember how we first heard of 'the Athens Bus' – but certainly once heard, not easily forgotten, for by comparison with all other forms of travel between Greece and Britain this was quite phenomenally the cheapest. At the time we were in Piraeus considering the economics of returning home a single air ticket from Athens to Heathrow was over £100, a trip by hired car would have cost much the same, and the second class railway fare was nearly £50. By comparison the single fare from Athens to Victoria Coach Station, London, on the Athens Bus, was £22!

If we had had any money to spare I at least would much prefer to have travelled by air, leaving Athens perhaps at 9 o'clock in the morning and being in London by mid-day: how swift and marvellously simple. But the sad fact was that the long trip had completely swallowed up all our available finances and it would be something of a miracle even if we could rustle up the bus tickets. Fortunately at long last Gina managed to sell her ring and raise enough money to cover one fare, and somehow I managed to collect enough to cover Stephen and Jess and myself. Thus armed I went into Athens and searched out the offices of one of the several tour operators who ran the weekly coach service.

'Here you are then,' said the attractive Greek girl clerk. 'Four seats on the coach from Athens to London, leaving Wednesday morning outside this office.' She smiled brightly. 'Please make sure you are here by a quarter to six.'

Groaning inwardly, for I hate early rising, I went off armed with a coloured brochure outlining immense almost tactical details of our forthcoming journey. Greece, Yugoslavia, Austria, West Germany, Belgium, England – 2000 miles through 6 countries at the astonishing rate of £1 per 100 miles! It sounded startling, adventurous, even rather exciting – but also, some warning voice sounded in my wise old head, probably something of an endurance test. You can say that again!

Perhaps the simplest thing is to give a blow by blow account of our epic journey, beginning at that grim grey dawn hour when a taxi deposited us outside the travel office, only to find some fifty or so other travellers already squatting on the pavement, mountains of luggage strewn all around. 'You may bring one suitcase and one travelling bag,' the girl had said warningly, but I could see that only a very tenuous lip service had been paid to that remark. We had been pretty cautious, but for a special reason. We carried with us Jess's large and ungainly donkey harness, which she was determined somehow to convey back to Land's End. This item, as I had feared, caused immediate trauma; the coach drivers threw up their hands in the air in disgust and went off to fetch the tour operator ... only after I had virtually threatened to lie down in protest in front of the coach did they relent and morosely stuff the harness deep into the luggage container.

Perhaps most surprisingly, although we were all there by a quarter to six in the morning the bus did not leave even by its advertised hour of six thirty. It took the drivers half an hour to pack all the luggage and then two girls discovered they were on the wrong coach, and everything had to be taken out and repacked. However around seven o'clock we were on the move, heading through the suburbs of Athens – where incidentally we picked up a party of eight Cypriot refugees, headed by a rather impressive old Greek Orthodox priest who sat solidly throughout the whole trip without once removing his tall clerical hat.

A word now about the coach. It was satisfactorily modern, powered by an excellent Mercedes Benz engine, and fitted out with reclining seats and (proudly advertised on the outside of the coach) air-conditioning. Unfortunately the luggage racks were very narrow so that much of the hand luggage would not fit in and had to be deposited here there and everywhere: a situation not improved by the arrival of the Cypriots plus most of their heavier luggage, for which there was no more room in the outside luggage containers. For those of us in the rear portion of the bus this entailed in all our comings and goings, considerable agility at stepping over water melons, wine casks, a sack of what looked like potatoes, and various large suitcases lining the only corridor. It says much for the general good humour prevailing that there were few cross words.

In this fairly confined space some 52 people of mixed nationalities, ages, classes, creeds, etc., endured each others very close proximity from 7 a.m., on the Wednesday morning, until 1.30 a.m., Saturday morning, when we reached Zeebrugge and transferred to the ferry steamer, and then for a further three hours on another coach from Dover to London. Most of the passengers were English, but there were also half a dozen Australians and about a dozen Americans, plus the Cypriots, a couple of Greeks and one or two Africans. Probably four-fifths of the passengers were young men and women in their early twenties, mostly student types (who we learned to identify in Greece as 'back-packers' because of the elongated tubular rucksacks which they humped around). Many of them were in pairs or groups, but it was evident that none of us had ever met before – possibly this (plus that famous British reticence) accounted for the fact that it took nearly three days for the ice to really break. By then everyone was on extremely matey terms, and we heard many a fascinating story of earlier adventures – driving a Volkswagen around Greece, working in a kibbutz in Israel, sailing on a charter yacht in the Aegean, getting caught in the war in Cyprus, and so on. Driving up from Dover on the last leg of the journey there were many expressions of regret that we had not started talking sooner!

The coach route was a simple if exhausting one. I quote from the brochure:

> Apart from Greece we will drive in Yugoslavia, Austria, West Germany and Belgium: we hope to cover the following distances: Greece, 580 kilometres, Yugoslavia, 1,000 kilometres, Austria, 340 kilometres, West Germany, 780 kilometres, Belgium, 270 kilometres. Estimated driving time in total is 45 hours not including overnight stops, and of course under normal traffic conditions. The route we follow is Athens – Nis – Belgrade – Stainach – Munich – Frankfurt – Cologne – Brussels – Zeebrugge – Dover – London.' And then a bland footnote: 'For the comfort of our passengers our drivers have been instructed to make comfort halts every four or five hours approximately for about 30-45 minutes each time.

'Comfort stops?' Well ...

Our first stop came at a small Greek town near the border.

'You have twenty minutes for coffee,' announced the chief driver, rather grudgingly it seemed to me as I began to stretch my numbed limbs. (After all *he* had a most comfortable seat, and beside him the co-driver had *the* most comfortable berth on the whole coach, a swivelling seat with a grandstand view in which he was able to doze in great comfort).

Being obviously an ardent Greek nationalist the driver went on to warn us that Yugoslavia was so expensive that we had better seize the opportunity to buy food in the local Greek food shops – 'and anyway the Yugoslavians are horrible people'. Too late we discovered that the Yugoslavs were delightful and friendly and their restaurants infinitely superior to anything we had seen in Greece. Also, returning to the 'comfort' theme, their toilets were a hundred per cent more civilised than the antiquated hole in the floor toilet which 52 of us queued up desperately in that forlorn Greek town. I am touching now, of course, on one of the fundamental problems of this confined form of travelling. On trains and planes and boats and almost every other form of travel, where toilets travel with you, there are no real problems ... on the Athens Bus, competing with 52 other equally desperate souls, the problem can be an acute one. The general reaction appeared to be universal constipation, and I suppose for $3\frac{1}{2}$ days this can be endured – but it is barely 'comfort'.

How the majority of the coach passengers managed to actually sleep overnight still confined to their seats I shall never quite know. Passengers are offered the chance of sleeping in hotels on the first two nights, and about fifteen of us thankfully grasped the opportunity. Our first night was spent in a very grand ultra modern hotel at Nis, in Yugoslavia – own private bathroom and toilet, luxury suite, the lot, all for just over £2 each, very pleasant. By contrast for the same sort of money, at Stainach in Austria we were piled 4 into a bedroom, unheated, and with a very distant single lavatory serving many people ... In the 'restaurant' we were offered a choice of goulash soup and goulash main course, and my plaintive request for a vegetarian's omelette was met by a brusque, 'No eggs. No cheese, you can have bread!'

Generally meals were no great problem as we invariably stopped outside a cafe of some sort, though sometimes at odd hours (the drivers used to have us up at 5 a.m. and get well on their way before the first stop – 'breakfast' might be at 10, 'lunch' was sometimes at 2.30 ... 'dinner' usually had to wait until our final arrival somewhere at about 10 p.m.) Our most expensive stop was at Munich in West Germany, just over 6 marks to the £1, and our cheapest and best meal of the trip was in a Belgian roadside cafe at the German-Belgium border, just over 50p a head including an excellent bottle of wine.

Getting the money to pay for the meals was another problem. Many of the students were obviously pretty broke but they seemed to manage by clubbing together. For those with money to change there were bureaux open at each of the frontiers.

Incidentally this brings me to one very positive advantage of travelling by the Athens Bus. Once our luggage had been so intricately packed away deep in the innards of the bus no customs officer, be he Greek, Yugoslavian, Austrian, German or Belgian, appeared willing to contemplate dragging it all out, and so nothing was inspected on the whole journey – except, needless to say, at Dover, and even that was very much a perfunctory inspection. ('And what do you think you've got there?' they said disapprovingly of Jess's strange parcel; but they allowed it to pass).

It was much the same with passports. At each frontier one of the drivers came round and collected our 52 passports and took them off to an office where they were most casually flipped through and returned – usually we were on our way in a quarter of an hour. It all makes nonsense of the whole antiquated passport system. Let us hope soon it perishes – in the meantime, for a determined smuggler the Athens Bus offers considerable possibilities!

How did the time pass? Well, we brought several paper backs, as did most of the other passengers, and there was a brisk trade in swapping, but for much of the time there was the outside world to provide entertainment. We certainly saw more of Europe than ever before, all in the space of three and a half days. We had 'done' Greece, but it remained barrenly beautiful to the end. After that Yugoslavia seemed incredible green and lush, though architecturally dull. Austria, by contrast, was full of aesthetic correctness, every house seeming to grow out of its locality, many of them quite beautiful – as for the landscape, it will be a long time before we forget waking up soon after dawn and looking our of our window to find we were high up in the mountains, surrounded by vast snow capped peaks. After that Germany seemed very flat, though bulging with prosperity ... Belgium we only glimpsed in the dark.

Once we reached Zeebrugge the drivers were obviously anxious to be rid of us: having thrust our ferry tickets into the hands of a 'volunteer' courier from among the passengers they bade hasty farewells, turned the coach round and were off on their way back to Athens. Probably in the busy season they pick up a fresh load of passengers going the opposite way, but this was late September and no doubt trade was slackening. Like most continentals our drivers were excitable and voluble, but there was no doubt that they were extremely skilful at their job, true professionals, and they kept us humming along at sixty miles an hour nearly all the way. In this they were helped by excellent roads nearly all the way, and the only real problem seemed the endless processions of double-length continental lorries. Heaven help England if they get a grip on our roads.

Just before reaching Zeebrugge the coach had made a brief stop on the outskirts of Brussels in order to drop off Stephen and Gina, who were returning to Paris – Gina to resume her ballet dancing, Stephen to have another go at busking in the Latin Quarter. Unfortunately by the time the bus reached Brussels not only was it after midnight, but also pouring with rain: and for Gina and Stephen, who planned to hitch-hike from Brussels to Paris, it cannot have seemed an inviting prospect. However, manfully Stephen shouldered his pack and his guitar case, and then Gina heaved up her own bag – and off they went, turning back to wave a last farewell just before the coach roared away.

Now that there were just the two of us Jess and I felt very alone. We sat together at the front of the Cross Channel Ferry, watching the sea all around us, seeming so different from those bright blue seas of our summer time cruising. Still, it was a calm enough crossing, and by dawn we were passing those famous white cliffs and backing into Dover Harbour.

Here there seemed to be an interminable wait before at last we found the coach hired by the tour company to take us the last stage of our journey. Typically we were met by a caricature of a phlegmatic English bus driver who patently couldn't care less about us or our fellow passengers, and was only prevailed upon most reluctantly to help load our luggage into the boot of the bus. We found ourselves almost wishing nostalgically for our Greek drivers! Still, only three hours and we were in Victoria Coach Station, what's more half an hour earlier than the time stated on the time-table. A quick dash by taxi to Paddington Station and by the skin of our teeth Jess and I managed to squeeze on the morning's Cornish Riviera.

Six hours later we were home and dry at The Mill House – donkey-harness and all!

XIII
And then there were Two

Autumn at the Mill House – about which we had often dreamed while basking in the hot Greek sunshine, thinking how much we would appreciate the lush green fields, the overhanging trees, the scents of all our English flowers – proved to be rather different from what we had rather too fondly imagined. True, initially we were immensely relieved to be back in such familiar surroundings, to be able to spread ourselves out in a way impossible on a boat, to throw open the bedroom window in the mornings and look out upon the wild green garden and the swaying trees – even to sit at breakfast and watch all the little chaffinches and tits fluttering around our bird bath. Ah, yes, England was a green and pleasant land, and Cornwall especially.

But this autumn, it wasn't exactly – that was the trouble. Come to think of it perhaps there had been a definite trend over several recent years … at any rate this autumn was far from pleasant. Green, yes, extra green, and that because of the incessant rains. During our absence abroad apparently the English summer had consisted very largely of rain – rain, rain and more rain. Now, as if especially for our benefit, autumn was repeating the pattern. On the very first morning after our return we heard the rain pattering on the roof: every day after three weeks, it just rained and rained *and* rained.

As if that wasn't enough to depress anyone – especially the suntanned travellers from the Greek Isles! – we were faced with other problems of adjustment. The greatest single one of them all was represented by Genevieve, or rather her sudden and rather final absence. Hitherto, over all the years, Jess and I had always had the company of one or more of our children to help provide a semblance, even if you like an illusion, of family life.

During the previous winter we had somehow got used to Genevieve being an integral part in our life – her daily arrival back from art school, signalled first by Roxy pricking up his ears and wagging his tail, then by the faint but increasingly louder phut-phut-phut of her Honda motor-cycle – at last the appearance in our glass doorway, like some traveller from outer space with her bright red helmet and old flying goggles and leather motoring coat, of Genevieve. No matter what we had been doing during the day, secretly Jess and I were awaiting that moment, the advent into our rather humdrum middle-aged lives of that bright-eyed golden girl.

Now, alas, six o'clock brought no barking of Roxy, no distant phutt-phutt – no golden girl. *She* was some 8000 miles away, high up in the Himalayan mountains. We had, of course the consolation of letters; in fact quite a stream of bright air mail epistles, for obviously Genevieve often felt rather home sick. Sometimes this nostalgia came through, and was almost unbearable. But often, too, we had to admit it sounded as if Genevieve was really enjoying herself. After all it must be a marvellous experience for any 20-year old English girl, suddenly to be transported into all the unfamiliar colourful surroundings of India's teeming continent.

At first Genny had stayed in Delhi, and we gathered she had found this not very pleasant, what with bodies of sleeping beggers strewing the streets and a general impression of considerable poverty. But then Sheldon took her up in the Himalayas, to a small village entirely taken over by Tibetan refugees, called Macleodbanj – and here, obviously, Genny felt much happier. She and Sheldon had managed to rent a chalet right up on the mountainside for £3 a month! – and here they proposed to spend several months while Sheldon showed his film of the Tibetan monks to the Dali Lama and other interested people, and also discussed some future films.

Genevieve, for her part, had an interesting and unexpected encounter. She was walking down the village street one day when who should she see but a young man, Jerry, whom she had last seen at a party at our former home, the Old Sawmills near Fowey! Apparently Jerry had become very interested in mysticism and Buddhism, and travelled out to India to find out for himself about these things. He had been living for several years in the locality and was very much as Genny put it, 'into' the Tibetan way of life. He had even fallen in love with a beautiful Tibetan girl and wanted to marry her – alas, her parents had 'arranged' her marriage to a fifty year old Tibetan and that *karma* could not be altered.

I couldn't help smiling a little at the grave way in which Genevieve presented these facts ... knowing how indignantly she would have rebelled against such a situation if I had tried to 'arrange' a marriage for her! All the same she was obviously growing very interested in the whole Tibetan way of life: in subsequent letters she told how she had struck up a great friendship with a Tibetan lady doctor, Amar Lobsang whose father had been a doctor in Lhassa, the capital of Tibet. In 1960 when the Chinese occupied Tibet she and her family, with thousands of other Tibetans, walked across the mountains into Napal, and eventually settled in Macloedeanj, where Amar Lobsang helped to run a large medical clinic.

Before long both Genny and Sheldon had become so friendly with Amar Lobsang that they were both experimenting with treatment from her – Sheldon for his poor eyesight, Genny for a long standing ovary trouble. In both cases the Tibetan lady doctor was using the ancient Chinese acupuncture method of treatment. Genevieve wrote a most interesting account of how this was done, with the use of a golden needle heated to burning point and then placed into various parts of the body. It didn't sound as far fetched as it might have done, as in recent years even in England the merits of acupuncture have been admitted – all the same we could not help worrying a bit. However, Genevieve wrote enthusiastically assuring us that both she and Sheldon felt quite rejuvenated.

This was just one instance of how Genevieve's education was being immensely broadened, and in a way it helped us better to put up with our own loss. But only partially – often we both felt quite bereft. In an attempt to take my mind off such problems I was able to plunge into a mountain of work awaiting for me: a series of yachting articles, a new book to write, another anthology to edit. At least I was fortunate enough to have such alternatives. Jess for her part had no such escape ... and so once again our sudden isolation, sense of being out in limbo, was brought back to us.

Jess, to do her justice, made herculean efforts to occupy herself. After all, there was that confounded donkey harness which had been brought back all of two thousand miles. It could hardly be left to rot in the hallway! One day – one rare day when the rain held off – Jess spent an hour or two finding out how the harness worked, then brought down Esmeralda, saddled her and embarked on a trial ride over to see our friend Biddy, at Glodgy Moor, Paul. I couldn't help feeling it was a rather ambitious journey, nearly seven miles, but Jess seemed quite confident.

Later that day I had a depressed phone call from Paul, where a somewhat shaken Jess had finally arrived after *walking* the whole 7 miles with a recalcitrant Esmeralda on a lead. Apparently, perhaps because of the recent continuous rains (donkeys hate rain) Esmeralda, usually so mild tempered, had been in a foul mood. Probably, too, she did not appreciate the donkey harness, which was quite heavy even on its own. Each time Jess had sat on the saddle Esmeralda had behaved most uncharacteristically, kicking her heels and so forth. As a consequence Jess had been thrown three times – the third time being quite a bad fall, banging her head on the hard road.

Jess explained on the phone how Biddy had given her a reviving drink and made her a meal, and now proposed to accompany her on the long walk back. Perhaps I would like to meet them on the way?

I did just that, coming along by the more mundane conveyance of an old Austin-Cambridge. Paradoxically, by then Esmeralda was on her best behaviour, so much so that

Biddy was now completely sold on the idea of having a donkey, and proposed in the near future to buy Lulu from us! Shaking my head in bafflement, I had to turn the car round and leave the two donkey-girls to their pleasure, for they were both quite happy to continue wandering along, taking it in turns to ride on the famous harness – which, apparently put you high up in the world, so that you got quite a new aspect of country life.

Yes, I suppose it might be said, in retrospect, that the donkeys helped to provide Jess with a certain continuing interest. So, of course, did the lives of our various children, which, thank goodness, were always on the change. That of our eldest, Martin, had recently taken a turn for the worse. Against his better judgement he had decided to leave his familiar haunts of Cornwall for the higher wages of London, where he had worked for some printing firm for a while, but it had all gone wrong – including, alas, his seemingly happy relationship with Karen – and now he was back in Cornwall rather a lost soul, living temporarily with us until he moved into a more permanent room in a friend's house in Penzance. Fortunately he managed to get back into printing jobs in Cornwall: gradually, as he began taking up the threads of life again, organising folk concerts, among old friends, we liked to think that life would perk up again for Martin.

Up in London our daughter Jane was going from success to success at the BBC, where as a film editor she seemed to be constantly hobnobbing with famous names. We could do nothing but applaud her enterprise, marvel at her very large salary, wish her well. Gill, her eldest sister, had not been so lucky lately. On returning from the *Sanu* cruise she had been a little put out to be laid off by the Chelsea Pottery, where she had worked for some years. However after a few weeks of frustration she had landed a job with the Pot Shop at Islington where she was soon in the heart of things, helping not only to sell pottery but to make stuff of her own. She was also doing some design jobs, and once again a busy little bee. Both she and Alan – who was making a determined effort to achieve something as a painter in his own right rather than a teacher –

were living a new sort of life, as after nearly ten years their spastic child, Emmy, had finally gone into a residential home. Obviously both Gill and Alan missed her terribly – equally obviously Emmy was very happy among other children, and the situation was something that now had to be accepted.

And then there was Demelza. She had been much in my thoughts lately because of a piece of good news I had received. Some years back, when Jess and I spent half a year in Bermuda, while Jess did a temporary job helping to organise a local pottery I had passed the time by writing a comic novel based loosely on Demelza. It was called *Don't Lose your Cool, Dad*, and as its title implied was written around the idea of a harassed father trying to cope with a series of bizarre situations in which he becomes involved through the over enthusiastic life style of his daughter. At the time the novel seemed very funny to myself and to Jess, to whom I would read each day's episode from the pen so to speak. Alas, several publishers had not seemed to agree, and I had begun to wonder if the novel would ever see the light of day.

Then recently, much to my delight a new firm which had started publishing my fiction, Milton House Books, decided they liked the book, and wrote accepting it for publication.

So it had given me great pleasure to be able to write and tell Demelza that the book she had inspired really was on the way. Meantime her own flamboyant life had continued to sparkle, with material enough for several new books. In particular, rather to our relief, she seemed to have settled down quite purposefully to a musical career, spending hours every day practising her bongas and tombas. We had been told by several experienced observers that Demelza was now quite brilliant on these instruments, so we kept hoping to hear of some dramatic progress.

At first Demelza concentrated on the idea of collecting together several other girl musicians and forming an 'all chicks' band. Once, I remember, we were asked to suggest names for the band, and camp up with Andromeda and Medusa, neither of them bad at all. The band did get formed and a demonstration tape was made of tunes which they composed themselves, which seemed to our outsiders' ears pretty good: but there were some kind of internal arguments and eventually the whole thing disintegrated.

Fortunately about this time Demelza had a real breakthrough ... the Theatre Upstairs, at the Royal Court Theatre, in Sloane Square, were putting on a six week run of a play by one of the more promising younger dramatists, Heathcote Williams, in which there was a small band involved – and a tomba player was needed. The idea of a *girl* tomba player appealed to Ken Campbell, the organiser. Demelza was recommended, went along for an audition – and rang us up excitedly to say she had got the job. This was great news indeed.

Of Stephen, the other musician in our family, we had heard hardly a word since that rainy night he and Gina left us at Brussels, hitching their way to Paris. This was mainly because of the seemingly never ending French postal strike which blotted out communications until nearly Christmas time. Just before the strike began we had had a brief note to say that Stephen was back at the busking – but we had paid less attention to that part of the note than to the latter section in which he had mentioned casually that Gina was expecting a baby the following May.

A baby? Stephen a father? It required a good deal of assimilating ... by the time we had really taken it in the post strike had struck up between us and so we did not know any further details. Fortunately during that period one or two friends from Cornwall called in at Paris and brought back glowing news of Stephen playing the cinema queues and earning himself quite a good living, indeed one friend said that he was now 'King of the Buskers'. Of Gina there was little more news – but the arrival at the Mill House of one or two 'posted very early' parcels from her parents in America made it self evident that by Christmas, at least we could expect a grand reunion.

From which, sad to say, the remaining and last of our six children would be – for the first time in twenty years – sadly absent. We still, thank goodness, heard regularly from

Genevieve, who by now had left Macleodganj and returned briefly to Delhi, where Sheldon had been putting the finishing touches to new plans. This time they were going off to Nepal – indeed to the legendary city of Katmandou, where Genny would be spending Christmas. Well, if she had to be away from the family hearth at least she was doing it in style.

However, what excited us in Genevieve's most recent letters – in fact in two or three long epistles from Sheldon, too – was not the news of their travels, interesting as that was. No, it was something else that looked as if it might involve us, too. Apparently ever since his rather alarming day's sail with us in *Sanu* Sheldon had been unable to get over the whole experience – that and the subsequent days living aboard in Piraeus. It had seemed to him that sailing in *Sanu* was a unique experience.

Now suddenly he had come up with his exciting new idea. Would we be interested in his making a film about our next *Sanu* cruise? What he had in mind was a kind of intimate documentary which would not merely be about the exterior delights of cruising, but about the family life aboard – including all the traumas! Waxing eloquently about his idea Sheldon threw in various ideas. Had we any old cine films of our early days on *Sanu*? He thought it would make an excellent opening for the film to have shots from several of these giving a kaleidoscopic impression of those early days – then suddenly cutting to a view of us all getting off an aeroplane at Athens Airport, all ready to start the next cruise ... Opening of Film!

Sheldon went into immense professional detail about what would need to be done. First he would write a treatment outlining the probable sequences in the film, a description of characters, etc. There would need to be timetable, budget, photos of all the participants, and then he would put up the whole scheme to potential backers. He felt sure that the film could be arranged – as he saw it it would be made by himself and Genevieve and one cameraman – the latter would have instructions *never* to get involved in any of the sudden situations that might arise, but always to be ready to film whatever happened.

'I must say it's a marvellous idea,' said Jess, reading Sheldon's enthusiastic letter. 'Where would we go? What about sailing to Cairo in search of my cousins, the Bryans of Cairo?'

'Well, maybe ... That would depend on the Suez Canal opening again.'

I wasn't personally madly keen on Jess's suggestion; and anyway Sheldon wrote back incisively in his next letter:

'Suez isn't essential, it would be exciting enough just cruising around the Greek Isles.'

This is how I felt too. Indeed, looking back on our recent trip I could see at once several episodes that would have made excellent film material. The night at Siphnos when the anchor dragged, the time at Seriphos when we were trapped for three days on the buoy, Alan and Stephen and Gina climbing over the mountains – the engine break down off Aegina, the gears jamming as we came into Piraeus – why there were endless incidents. We could even, surely, re-stage some of them? Well, it was a thought! Though in fact I knew perfectly well there would be no need to go to such artificial lengths, every *Sanu* trip brought its own traumatic incidents, of that we could be sure.

After receiving Sheldon's letter Jess and I felt a little more cheerful. Suddenly there was one thing at least to plan for. We were uplifted, too, in a curious way, by the streams of philosophical letters that continued to come from Genevieve.

I just cannot conceive where everything began. I read books and words, all of them saying different things, but no difference. I see people searching for different visions, but no different. I myself am sad happy greedy lazy kind cruel empty full, but no different than the rest of mankind. I'm aware of life itself, or I think I am, looking down at my hands, seeing the beauty in the living physical self. I'm aware, too, of many fine wise masters on this earth who seem to know what it's all about. I know how to laugh at it all too, when I see how futile it all becomes. Have you both found happiness with your lives? Is each moment just a memory or part of the intricate pattern of man's life that binds our concepts of what existance is? Will I be told I must not think like this, I must just live and be content? I'm not content because if I can think of the question, there must be an answer. Oh I don't know how many thousands of years, how many pointless tears have drowned us. Who am I writing for? Who am I painting for? What does it matter if someone says it's good or bad? Is life worth living because of what I put into it or for what it gives me? I was taught in school I must give to receive. I seem only to have received the knowledge that I must be creative, work for my life, pretend everything has always been, is, and forever will remain so. How very easy it all is to smile. All these words don't build me a bridge to cross over, they only drown me with sorrow. Look at mankind, look at its blindness, yet we were tireless through its filth searching, believing that one day we'll know. I've seen love even used as a religion, 'I'm in love so I no longer care' is how it goes. I wish I were simple then I would just be real. I feel empty and false, I seem to be playing a part. I'd rather be a flower in your garden. I keep seeing myself getting older but still filling myself up with more confusion, more words that lead me in circles. A cup with a hole in, I never learn. I just don't believe that I have anything special to give because I seem so vague so stupid, it's all an act so people won't see how empty I am. I surround myself with painting writing music, for an image, take it away and there's someone called Genny who doesn't know how to give or love, who's lost in this sad world. I can love though, that's what keeps me alive is my love for you both, do you know you are my strength and my dreams? I hope you understand Genny's only truth is you.

Somehow, reading letters like that, realising that one of our own little flowers was suddenly opening out to all the world's mysterious wonders – gave us two weary old people a curious sense of uplift. I suppose you could call it, mundanely, 'living through one's children'. All I know is that now, deep in the heart of our rather lonely Cornish valley, we came to understand that we were not alone ... that distance was really no barrier, there were always fast cheap flights run on that limitless fuel known as love! How lucky we were really.

That autumn, the rains went on, the winter drew near ... but somehow we felt we would survive to another year, another summer. Ahead of us raced all kinds of exciting possibilities. Life was always there waiting to be lived. And even here, alone:

'Shall we take a walk to Nanjizel? I think the rain's stopping. You never know, it might clear – we could go on the cliffs and watch the sunset over the Scillies!